BOOK

DAVID BOLTON
CLIVE OXENDEN
LEN PETERSON

Oxford University Press

Oxford University Press
Great Clarendon Street, Oxford OX2 6DP

Oxford New York
Athens Auckland Bangkok Bogota Bombay
Buenos Aires Calcutta Cape Town Dar es Salaam Delhi
Florence Hong Kong Istanbul Karachi Kuala Lumpur
Madras Madrid Melbourne Mexico City Nairobi
Paris Singapore Taipei Tokyo Toronto

and associated companies in
Berlin Ibadan

OXFORD and OXFORD ENGLSIH
are trade marks of Oxford University Press

ISBN 0 19 432365 X

© Oxford University Press 1990

First published 1990
Fifth impression 1997

Typeset by Pentacor PLC, High Wycombe, Bucks

Printed in Hong Kong

The authors would like to acknowledge the help and cooperation of the
following schools in the production of this course:

Abon Language School, Bristol; Alos Centro Europeo de Idiomas,
Valencia; Anglo European Study Tours, London; IHSP, Bromley; ITS,
Hastings; Kings School, Beckenham; The British Institute, Valencia

and the following people at Oxford University Press:

Coralie Green, Jean Hindmarch, Claire Nicholl, Rosemary Nixon, James
Richardson, Greg Sweetnam, Katy Wheeler.

Special thanks also go to Paul Power, Fiona Wright, Carmen Dolz,
Beverley Johnson, Cristina Garcia Gomez, Hervé Goineau and Maria
Vicente.

Exercise 6 on p.59 is based on material from *Conversation* p.97, by
Rob Nolasco and Lois Arthur in the Resource Books for Teachers
Series, (OUP) 1987.

Words and music to *Streets of London* © 1968 Westminster Music
Ltd, Suite 2.07, Plaza 535 Kings Road, London, SW10 0SZ.
International Copyright Secured. All Rights Reserved. Used by
Permission.

Illustrations by:

Martin Chatterton, Tech Graphics, Robina Green, Gordon Hendry, Sian
Leetham, Mohsen/Funny Business, Christine Roche, Nick Sharrat.

The publishers would like to thank the following libraries for permission
to reproduce photographs:

Ace Photo Agency, All Action/Mark Leech, Aquarius Picture Library,
Barnaby's Picture Library, Anthony Blake, Britain on View (BTA/ETB),
Martyn Chillmaid, Greg Evans Photo Library, Hulton/Deutsch collection,
Image Bank/R. Lockyer, Last Resort Picture Library, Rex Features,
Spectrum Colour Library, Tony Stone Worldwide, Syndicaton
International, Telefocus/a British Telecom Photograph

and the following for their time and assistance:

Benetton SpA, The Boots Company PLC, The Eckersley School of
English, Marks and Spencer PLC, Midland Bank, Museum of Modern Art,
Next, Pizza Hut, The Post Office, WH Smith.

Studio and location photography by:

Paul Freestone, Mark Mason.

Stills photographer:

Rob Judges.

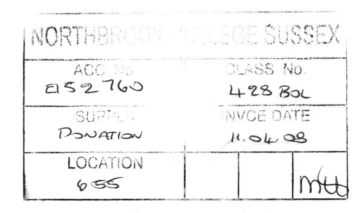

UNIT	LESSON I	LESSON 2	LESSON 3
	GRAMMAR IN ACTION	ENGLISH IN SITUATIONS	FUN WITH ENGLISH
1 PAGES 6–11	present simple/present continuous contrasted position of adverbs of frequency present continuous for future	introducing yourself and other people greeting people asking for things saying goodbye using public telephones making an international phone call	*Further practice in:* pronunciation listening vocabulary reading speaking finding out about the UK
2 PAGES 12–17	compounds with *some/any/no* *have to/don't have to* *must/mustn't* *(not) allowed to*	asking and talking about the price of things statistics asking about and telling the time	*Further practice in:* pronunciation listening vocabulary reading speaking finding out about the UK
3 PAGES 18–23	past simple/past continuous/past perfect contrasted reported speech	asking permission giving and refusing permission accepting and refusing food at mealtimes making offers apologizing and responding to apologies	*Further practice in:* pronunciation listening vocabulary reading speaking finding out about the UK
4 PAGES 24–29	*much/many/a lot/a few/ a little/plenty of/hardly any* question tags future: *will*	describing where buildings/ places are asking for and giving directions changing money cashing traveller's cheques	*Further practice in:* pronunciation listening vocabulary reading speaking finding out about the UK
5 PAGES 30–35	comparatives superlatives expressing preferences talking about numbers/ statistics	using the telephone taking and leaving telephone messages spelling in English	*Further practice in:* pronunciation listening vocabulary reading speaking finding out about the UK
6 PAGES 36–41	past simple/present perfect contrasted present perfect with *for/ since/already/yet/just/ever*	buying clothes talking about sizes and colours making complaints	*Further practice in:* pronunciation listening vocabulary reading speaking finding out about the UK

GRAMMAR IN ACTION

The best about Britain?

Every year, thousands of foreign students visit Britain. We asked some of them, 'What do you like best about Britain? These are some of their answers.

'The old people. They're so friendly, and they've nearly always got time to help you. When you don't know where you are, they come up to you and say, "Can I help you, love?" or "What are you looking for, dear?" I love the way they call everybody "love" and "dear" like that - even complete strangers.'

'Why does everybody say the weather here's so bad? I love these cool, grey, cloudy days. They're a bit sad - perhaps that's why I like them. I come from Turkey. It's sunny most of the time there, and I sometimes get fed up with it. But here the weather's so changeable. You hardly ever know what to expect when you look out of the window in the morning - and then it often changes five or six times during the day! It's raining now, for example, but I've got no idea what it's going to be like this afternoon!'

'I like the character of the people. Foreigners usually complain that the British are very reserved and distant. But I don't agree. I like the way they're always so calm and controlled, just like in films. If you tell a British person something really dramatic, like his house is on fire, he doesn't panic. He just calmly dials 999 and then sits down and has a cup of tea!'

'What do I like best about Britain? The fact that people here very rarely smoke. I never smoke myself - I think it's a disgusting habit. But my friends in Spain smoke nearly all the time. It's so nice to be able to breathe "clean" air in cinemas, on buses and so on. And the few people who do smoke, almost always ask "Do you mind if I smoke?" before they light up.'

'I'm staying with an English family. Family life here seems to be much more relaxed than in my country. People eat whenever they like, come in and go out whenever they want to - there aren't so many rules. When I go out in the evening, nobody asks me "Where are you going? Who are you going with? What time are you coming home?" You've got much more privacy, the chance to live your own life, and do whatever you want.'

I Class survey

Read the following statements:

A B C

1 The old people in Britain are friendly and helpful.
2 They usually call you 'dear' or 'love'.
3 The weather in Britain is usually grey and cloudy.
4 The weather can change five or six times during the day.
5 The British are not reserved and distant.
6 The British are always calm and controlled.
7 Smokers ask if they can light up.
8 Very few people in Britain smoke.
9 Family life in Britain is more relaxed than in other countries.
10 There are more rules in Britain and there is less privacy than in other countries.

a Tick (√) your own answers (A, B, or C).

A = I agree.
B = I don't know./I'm not sure.
C = I don't agree.

b Ask each other the questions in small groups. Make notes of your results.

c Compare your results with those of other groups. Work out the total number of students who agree and disagree with each statement. Write up the results in a short paragraph.

2 What do they think of Britain?

Listen to some foreign students talking about what they like or don't like about Britain.

Fill in the missing information. There is an example first.

Example:

Nationality	Best thing	Worst thing
Example: Spanish	the postal service	
1	....	....
2	....	....
3	....	....
4	....	....
5	....	....
6	....	....

3 Grammar practice

Complete the following dialogue. Think of suitable verbs and put them in the right tenses. Choose between:

the present simple
(*I live in London.*)

the present continuous
(*I'm staying with an Irish family.*)

the present continuous for future.
(*I'm going to Brighton tomorrow.*)

A What (you) . . . tonight?
B I . . . a friend. We . . . the cinema.
A What time . . . film?
B At 8.15.
A I (not) . . . anything this evening. . . . I . . . too?
B Yes, of course you . . .
A Where (you) . . . ?
B At the bus station at 8.
A OK, there's a bus which . . . there at 7.50.
B I'd better go. I . . . with a very strict family, and we . . . supper at half past six. See you later.

4 Make sentences

Write sentences putting the words in the correct order.

Example:
got have you help people to always time
People have always got time to help you.

1 are calm always people nearly English
2 ask going they you where never are
3 fed up the I get sometimes weather with
4 the disco go always they same to almost
5 in hardly cinemas smoke ever people nowadays

5 Quick questions

In five minutes, find as many students as you can:

• whose first name has the same number of letters as yours.
• whose surname ends with the same letters as yours.
• who was born in the same year as you.
• whose birthday is in the same month as yours.
• who wears the same size shoes as you do.
• whose telephone number ends with the same number as yours.
• who uses the same kind of toothpaste as you do.
• who has the same number of spoonfuls of sugar in their tea or coffee as you do.
• who has a watch which was made in the same country as yours.
• who's wearing the same colour socks as you.

The 'winner' is the student with the most names after five minutes.

Grammar summary: page 82

7

1 Greetings, introductions and saying goodbye

A Hi, Paul. How are things?
B Not bad. You haven't met my girlfriend, have you? This is Ulrike. Ulrike, Chris.
A Hi, nice to meet you . . . Sorry, what was your name again?
C Ulrike.
A Ulrike – that's difficult!
C Most people call me Rikki for short.
A Yeah, that's a bit easier. Anyway, I've got to dash. See you around. Have a good time in England, Rikki.
C Thanks. Bye bye.
B Cheers, Chris. See you soon.

Practise the dialogue in groups of three using your own names and substituting the phrases below.

How are you?	OK, thanks.
How's it going?	Not too bad.
How's life?	All right, thanks.
How are you doing?	Fine.

I'd better go now.	I'm in a hurry.
I must be off now.	I've got to rush.
	again.
See you	tomorrow.
	on Monday.

2 Formal introductions

A Alan, I'd like you to meet Christine Evans.
B How do you do? Pleased to meet you.
C How do you do, Mr Stewart? I've heard a lot about you.

Practise the dialogue in groups of three.

3 Asking for things

A Can I have a grapefruit juice, please?
B Sorry?
A A grapefruit juice, please.
B With ice?
A Yes, please.
B Anything else?
A No, thanks.

C Could I have a front door key, please?
D Beg your pardon?
C Can I have a key, please?
D Yes, of course . . . Here you are.

a Practise the dialogues in pairs.

b Think of things you would ask for in the following shops and places. Improvise dialogues asking for the things you thought of. Change roles.

MARKS & SPENCER

WH SMITH

Pizza Hut

Post Office

Boots

benetton

4 Telephoning

Using public telephones

1	2

1   This is a coin-operated payphone. There are instructions next to the telephone telling you how to make a call. There is a 'window' where you can see how much money you have left. Some phones have a 'follow-on call' button. Press it if you want to make more than one call with the money you put in.

2   This is a Cardphone, which does not take coins. Buy a phone card at post offices or shops where you see the phonecard sign.

Read the instructions and put them in the right order.

☐ Dial the number you want. The digital display will show the number of unused units on the card. Listen for the ringing tone and speak when connected.

☐ Retrieve the card.

☐ Lift the receiver and listen for the dialling tone.

☐ When you finish your call, replace the receiver.

☐ Insert the card into the slot, green side up, in the direction of the arrow.

How to make an international call

1   Dial 010.

2   Dial the code for your country.

    Examples:
    France 33   Italy 39   Spain 34
    Germany 49   Japan 81   Brazil 55

3   Now dial the code for the town/city you want (usually without the first figure).

    Examples:
    Athens 1   Stockholm 8   Barcelona 3

4   Finally, dial the number of the person you want to speak to.

Write down the full number of your own family (or a friend in your country) if you want to phone them from Britain.

5 ☺ What do they want?

Listen to the short dialogues on the cassette. Fill in the missing information. There is an example first.

	Where?	What?	How much?
	post office	stamp	49p
1			
2			
3			
4			
5			

Summary of English in situations

● greeting people
● introducing yourself and other people
● saying goodbye
● asking for things
● using public telephones
● making an international phone call

I 📼 Sound right

a Work in pairs. Student A looks at the words below, student B at the words on page 78.

two	laugh	filled
short	see	bank
sun	bed	put
were	hot	

b Ask student B 'Which of your words rhymes with . . . ?' Take it in turns to ask and answer. Write down the rhyming pairs.

c Now listen and repeat the pairs of words on the cassette.

d Think of more rhyming words, at least one for each pair.

Example:
hot – what – shot

2 Language games

Think of a sentence

a Form two teams, A and B.

b The teacher says a letter, for example, S. One member of team A must make a sentence with a noun and an adjective both beginning with S. A member of team B then thinks of another sentence. The teacher writes the sentences on the board.

Example:

Team A *Strawberries are sweet.*
Team B *Sheep are stupid.*

This continues until one team can't think of another sentence (there is a time limit of five seconds.) The team who said the last sentence score a point.

c The teacher says a new letter and the game continues.

3 Work on words

Which one of the five alternatives does not go with the verb on the left?

Example:							
break	a leg a promise a record a meeting a window	3 get	a letter angry home brown wrong	6 pay	a bill a visit attention cheque your debts
I catch	a bus a cold fire a fish a holiday	4 make	a mistake a favour money arrangements friends	7 do	your homework your hair a phone call business your best
2 tell	a lie the truth goodbye the time a joke	5 have	a shower cold an argument a chat fun	8 take	a decision care of somebody notice of somebody the sun an aspirin

4 Time to talk

a Work in groups. In your groups, think up a story. You must include all these things and people. Make notes as you decide what happens.

b The members of each group tell the story to the rest of the class.

5 Read and think

Read the following notices and extracts from newspapers carefully. There is something wrong with each item. Sometimes it's a spelling mistake, sometimes an absurdity. Explain and correct the mistakes.

Example:

> A thrilling film story of ten men lost in the dessert

Answer: *There is a spelling mistake, 'dessert' should be 'desert'.*

1	In the sixth form we've been trying to get rid of school uniform. I think we'll get to the point soon where the boys just wear a tie and the girls a grey skirt.	6	Au pair wanted, 2 adults, 2 young children. Modern flat, own bedroom. Centrally heated student ideal. Tel: 45332.
2	LOST — dog. Only has three legs. Blind in left eye. Right ear missing. Tail broken. Answers to the name of 'Lucky'.	7	The children threw roses as the General walked past. Two schoolgirls presented him with a large bouquet of flowers. 'God bless you, my children, and thank you,' he said, as he killed them both.
3	During her next tour the Queen will travel by goat.	8	For Sale - English bulldog. Will eat anything. Very fond of children. £35.
4	**POLICE FOUND SAFE UNDER BLANKET**	9	Mr and Mrs Jackson request the honour of your presents at the wedding of their daughter Julia.
5	Unemployed man seeks work. Completely honest and trust—worthy, will take anything.	10	Staff members should empty the teapot and then stand upside down on the the tray.

6 Listen to this

You need a piece of paper and a pen. Follow the instructions carefully and then listen to the solution.

7 Now you're here

a Find out about the town/city/area you're staying in. Ask a British person to help you.

Name of the town/city/area
Population
Distance from central London
Tourist attractions
Famous historical figures/events
Main industry
Name and party of local MP
Best football team
Most popular club/disco
Opening/closing times of shops
Early closing day

b Which of these buildings/facilities are there? Mark each of them with a tick (√) or cross (×).

1	a cathedral	☐
2	a museum	☐
3	an amusement arcade	☐
4	a market	☐
5	a castle	☐
6	an ice rink	☐
7	a university	☐
8	an art gallery	☐
9	a pier	☐
10	a bowling alley	☐
11	a concert hall	☐
12	a library	☐
13	a sports centre	☐
14	a hospital	☐
15	a cinema	☐
16	a theatre	☐
17	a swimming pool	☐
18	a technical college	☐
19	a prison	☐
20	a tourist information office	☐

c Now mark them on a local map.

GRAMMAR IN ACTION

🖾 Dressed for work

You can't always wear what you want. These three people all have to wear a kind of uniform.

Sarah Hopkins is a sales assistant at a branch of Next.

Mick Roberts is a bouncer at a London nightclub. His 'uniform' is a dinner jacket and a bow tie.

Charlotte Russell is eighteen. She's in the sixth form at school.

'I have to wear clothes from the shop while I'm at work. I suppose I'm a sort of walking advertisement! But I don't have to pay the full price - the store gives us a clothes allowance, and then we get a 30 to 50 per cent discount on everything we buy.

My friends envy me because my clothes are always in fashion. And I'm lucky because I don't have to wear something different for work and for going out somewhere, like a disco or a party.'

'I always have to look smart, like this, at work, because if someone's wearing jeans or hasn't got a tie, I'm the one who has to tell him he can't come in. When somebody gets a bit over-excited or aggressive, I have to throw him out. And sometimes my clothes get torn or messed-up.

I'm not allowed to wear jewellery, because anything loose can get caught in a customer's clothes when I'm "escorting" him out.

Nobody could call it a boring job. Anything can happen on a Saturday night!'

'I had to wear a strict school uniform until I was 16. Now I don't have to but we still can't wear whatever we like. We're not allowed to wear anything too extreme or too fashionable. For example, there was a girl who came to a French class one morning in a T-shirt, mini-skirt and high heels. The teacher sent her straight out. But among my friends I can't think of anybody who'd wear clothes like that, I suppose we just prefer something more stylish.'

1 Ask questions

a Form small groups. Each group thinks of nine questions about Sarah, Mick and Charlotte (three for each). Everybody writes them down.

b Each student finds a partner from a different group. Take it in turns to ask your questions. Answer without looking in the book.

2 Grammar practice

Complete the following sentences. Use *have (has) to, mustn't,* or *don't (doesn't) have to* and *not allowed to*.

1 Sarah . . . wear clothes from the shop all the time.
2 Charlotte . . . wear a mini-skirt at school.
3 I . . . be in the office until ten o'clock today, so I can stay in bed longer.
4 I really . . . go now, I'm half an hour late.
5 You . . . drive down there, it's a one-way street!
6 Mick . . . work during the day, he begins work at 8 p.m.

3 What's missing?

a Complete the dialogue with:

some somebody something somewhere
any anybody anything anywhere
no nobody nothing nowhere

A I want to go (1) . . . different tonight. (2) . . . except the Minerva Club!

B You know we can't go (3) . . . We haven't got (4) . . . money.

A Well, can't we borrow (5) . . . from your sister? You can make (6) . . . excuse you like, she always believes you.

B There's (7) . . . chance.

A Oh well, it doesn't really matter, I haven't got (8) . . . to wear.

B You're joking! You're wearing (9) . . . new every time I see you. (10) . . . I know has got as many clothes as you. That's why you've got (11) . . . money.

A You're right, I suppose, but I haven't bought (12) . . . this week.

b Now practise the conversation in pairs.

4 What are they allowed to do?

a 📺 Listen to three foreign students, Michel, Enrica, and Hans who are staying with British families. Write down what they say about:

- coming home at night
- smoking
- being on time for meals
- having baths
- using the phone.

b Compare your answers in groups. Then discuss the 'rules' in your British family, or in your family at home. Talk about the same things as you heard on the cassette, but include other problems as well.

Use these words and phrases:

can can't (not) allowed to
(don't) have to must(n't)

Example:
Michel. *He's not allowed to come home after 12 o'clock.*

5 Laws

a How old do you have to be in your country to:

- leave school?
- ride a moped or scooter?
- drive a car?
- buy cigarettes?
- buy alcohol?
- leave home (if your parents agree)?
- have a part-time job?
- marry without your parents' permission?
- be tattooed?
- give blood?
- vote in elections?
- donate part of your body to save other people's lives (without your parents' permission)?

b Work in pairs. Ask each other 'How old do you have to be in your country to . . . ?' Do you agree with the age limits?

6 Noughts and crosses

Write this word square on the board.

something	anywhere	no
anybody	somebody	nothing
nobody	nowhere	anything

a Form two teams, O's and X's.

b Team O choose a square. In less than 15 seconds they must think of a sentence using the word in that square.

Example:
Nobody I know smokes.

If the sentence is correct, a member of team O rubs out *nobody* and replaces it with an *O*. If the sentence is wrong, *nobody* stays and can be used again.

c Team X then choose a square and think of a correct sentence in the same way.

The idea is for each team to make a line of O's or X's, across, down or diagonally.

Grammar summary: page 82

1 Using British money

How much is this?

a Work in pairs. Ask and answer questions about each picture.

Example:
A *How much is this?*
B *It's £1.66.*

1

2

3

4

b Now say how much the coins in each picture are worth in your currency.

2 What do you need?

a Work in pairs. Look at the things in the picture. What is the minimum number of coins you need to pay for them exactly? Take it in turns to ask and answer.

Example: 18p

A *How many coins do you need to buy this orange?*
B *Four coins – 10p, 5p, 2p and 1p.*

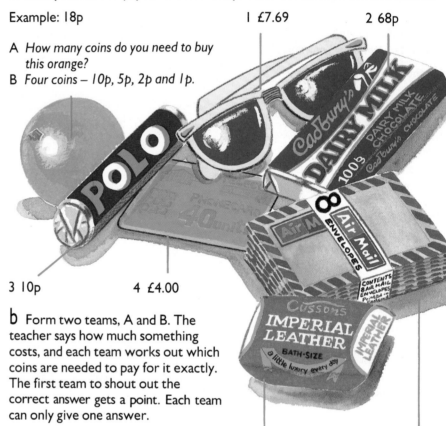

1 £7.69   2 68p

3 10p   4 £4.00

5 57p   6 £1.22

b Form two teams, A and B. The teacher says how much something costs, and each team works out which coins are needed to pay for it exactly. The first team to shout out the correct answer gets a point. Each team can only give one answer.

Example:
Teacher *£1.63.*
Team A *One pound, fifty p, ten p, and two twos.*
Team B *No, one pound, fifty p, ten p, two p and one p.*

3 How much is it?

A *Can I have a Coke and a chicken sandwich, please?*
B *Anything else?*
A *No, thanks. How much is that?*
B *That's . . . um . . . 82p, please. Thank you. That's 18p change.*
A *Thanks.*

a Practise the dialogue in pairs.

b Improvise similar dialogues using the things and prices in the picture in Exercise 2 above.

4 ▣ How do you say it?

a Listen to how you say the following and repeat after the cassette.

£3.99	9.83 secs
£78.95	15.5%
£493.45	$9 + 1 - 3 = 7$
£236,000	$4\frac{1}{3}$
129,432,311	$7\frac{2}{3}$
1901–1912	$\frac{1}{2} + \frac{1}{4} = \frac{3}{4}$
Tues. – Thur.	$100°F = 38°C$
21/7/71	$12 \div 3 \times 2 = 8$
22nd – 31st August	Spurs 3 QPR 0
5' 8"	6–2, 3–6, 6–0
1.78m	

b Now listen to the cassette and write down the numbers and statistics you hear.

5 Asking about and telling the time

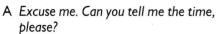

A *Excuse me. Can you tell me the time, please?*
B *Yes, it's just after half past three.*
A *Thanks.*

C *Have you got the time on you?*
D *Oh, yes, it's nearly ten o'clock.*
C *Thanks very much.*

Practise the dialogues in pairs. Then take it in turns to ask and say what time it is, using the times below.

6 What time is it?

Listen to some short conversations and announcements. Write down the times you hear in each of them. There is an example first.

Example: *5.15*

1 ....

2 ....

3 ....

4 ....

5 ....

6 ....

Summary of English in situations
• asking and talking about the price of things
• statistics
• asking about and telling the time

1 📼 Sound right

a Listen to these pairs of words on the cassette.

it	eat	man	men	cat	cut
fit	feet	sat	set	match	much
live	leave	bad	bed	ran	run

What's the difference in pronunciation between the vowel sounds?

b Now listen again and repeat the pairs of words.

c Listen to different pairs of words on the cassette. Put a tick (√) if the two words are the same, and a cross (×) if they're different.

Example: ☒

1 ☐   4 ☐   7 ☐
2 ☐   5 ☐   8 ☐
3 ☐   6 ☐   9 ☐

2 Language games

Mini-crosswords

a Form teams.

b The teacher writes a word on the board, for example, NIGHT. In two minutes each team has to think of related words using each letter in night.

Example:

Nightdress
PIllow
Ghost
NigHtmare
MaTtress

c The first team to finish get one point. The words must be spelt correctly.

3 Work on words

Each word in the box on the right goes with another word. The two words are usually joined by *and*.

Example:
ladies and gentlemen

Write out the phrases. Make sure the words are in the right order.

sausage	pains	bed
paper	butter	peace
sweet	chalk	tie
ends	milk	lemon
buts	socks	eggs
lightning	ladies	odds
jacket	bacon	sugar
coffee	ice	pen
breakfast	quiet	tea
shoes	sour	aches
bread	cheese	if
gentlemen	thunder	mash

4 Time to talk

Work in pairs. Student A reads the instructions below and student B reads the instructions on page 78.

Look at the picture below. Student B has a similar picture but with ten differences. Describe your picture to student B. Student B will describe his/her picture to you. Try to find the ten differences.

5 Read and think

a The poems below are called limericks. The last line always rhymes with the first and second lines. Read the limericks and try to complete the last line for each one. You may need one, two or three words.

Example:
There was an old man from Peru,
Who dreamt he was eating his shoe,
He woke up in the night,
With a terrible fright,
And discovered it really **was true**.

There was a young man from Devizes,
Whose ears were of different sizes.
The one that was small
Was no good at all
But the other won . . .

There was an old man from Darjeeling,
Who travelled from London to Ealing,
It said on the door,
Please don't spit on the floor,
So he got up and . . .

There was a young man from Rangoon
Who said, 'I shall fly to the moon.'
So upwards he went,
But the rocket was bent,
So he came back . . .

I'd rather have fingers than toes,
I'd rather have ears than a nose,
And as for my hair,
I'm glad it's still there,
I'll be terribly sad . . .

b 📼 Compare your limericks with the rest of the class then listen to the complete limericks on the cassette.

6 📼 Listen to this

One-sided conversation

a Listen to a telephone conversation on the cassette. You only hear what one of the people says.

b Listen again, line by line. In pairs write down what you think the other person says.

c Now listen to the whole conversation and compare your dialogue with the one on the cassette.

7 Now you're here

Find out the answers to these questions.

1 What time do banks open/close?
2 How much does a first class stamp cost?
3 How much does it cost to send a postcard to your country?
4 What number do you dial if you want the police or an ambulance?
5 What's the dialling code for London?
6 After what time is it cheaper to phone abroad?
7 What's the name of the local evening paper?
8 Are the following cheaper or more expensive in Britain than in your country?
 a CD
 a Mars bar
 hiring a tennis court
 a blank cassette
 renting a video
 a pair of Levi jeans
9 How much is VAT?
10 What record is number 1 in Britain at the moment?
11 Name three products from your country which you can buy in Britain.

UNIT THREE
LESSON ONE

No Exit

The residents of an old people's home near Cambridge complained because local children were playing in their garden. They asked the owners of the home to put up a fence to keep the children out. The owners agreed.

Two days later, a lorry arrived with three workmen. They worked hard for four days and the fence was almost finished.

'I was watching them from my window,' said Emily Watkins, a resident. 'They were just finishing the fence, when one of them suddenly realized that they'd forgotten something. They hadn't left a gap in the fence to get their lorry out.'

The man in charge of the job said later they'd been working very hard and hadn't noticed that there was no exit for the lorry.

We all make mistakes

The Wrong Day

When George Lewis, an experienced shoplifter, went into a department store in Poole, he wasn't expecting too many problems. There were several other customers in the shop and he waited until he thought no one was looking and then began putting things into his bag. But as he was walking out of the shop, five pairs of hands suddenly grabbed him from behind.

The store detective asked him to go back into the shop and then told him to open his bag. It contained three shirts, two pairs of trousers and a leather jacket. The store manager asked him where his receipt was and he said he didn't have one.

'I couldn't find a changing room free, so I was taking the clothes home to try them on,' he said.

Five minutes later he admitted that he had stolen the clothes. The police arrived and arrested him.

The manager of the store later commented that the thief had not chosen a very good day to shoplift. 'We were holding a training course for new store detectives. He didn't stand a chance - there were twenty of them!'

1 Four interviews

a Work in pairs. One of you (A) is a newspaper reporter, the other (B) is George Lewis. A has his/her book open, B has his/her book closed.

A asks questions using the word prompts below, B answers them.

Example:
A *When did you put things in your bag?*
B *When I thought no one was looking.*

A *When / (put) things / bag?*
B ...
A *What (happen) / (leave)?*
B ...
A *What / (be) excuse?*
B ...
A *What / (admit) later?*
B ...
A *What / police (do) / (arrive)?*
B ...

b Change roles so that B (a newspaper reporter) asks the questions, and A (the store detective who interviewed Lewis) answers them.

B *Why (be) / Poole?*
A ...
B *How many / (be) training course?*
A ...
B *What / (take)?*
A ...
B *Where / (put) things?*
A ...
B *Where / (stop) him?*
A ...
B *Where / (be) receipt?*
A ...
B *When / (admit) / (steal) clothes?*
A ...

c A is a newspaper reporter. He/she interviews Mrs Watkins (B). Improvise the whole dialogue.

d B is now the reporter interviewing A (the man in charge of building the fence). Improvise the whole dialogue.

2 📼 What happened?

Listen to the sounds on the cassette and write down what *was happening* (past continuous) when something else *happened* (past simple). Make notes first with the help of the words below. Then write a complete sentence. There is an example first.

Example: thumb
He was hammering in a nail when he hit his thumb.

1 joke	6 knock over
2 cut off	7 hiccup
3 sneeze	8 run out of
4 snore	9 ceiling
5 TV	10 shower

3 Grammar practice

Find verbs to complete the following sentences using the past simple (for example, *went*), the past continuous (for example, *was going*) or the past perfect (for example, *had gone*).

Example:
I . . . going to the airport by taxi when I suddenly . . . that I . . . forgotten my passport.

I was going to the airport by taxi when I suddenly realized that I had forgotten my passport.

1 We . . . television when my cousin . . . to tell us she . . . £100,000 on the football pools.
2 The concert . . . when we . . . , but luckily our friends . . . outside with our tickets.
3 When the journalist . . . the scene of the accident, an ambulance . . . the injured people to hospital. A police officer . . . an eye witness.
4 I . . . home late last night. My mother . . . to bed, but my father . . . in the sitting room.
5 We . . . in the garden when the fire alarm . . . off. We . . . a pan on the cooker and it . . .

4 What did he say?

Paola is telling Regina what Richard, an English boy she met, said to her last night. Read the first part and continue Paola's story.

'What's your name?'
'Where are you from?'
'How long have you been in England?'

Well, he asked me what my name was and where I was from. Then he asked how long I had been in England.

'How old are you?'
'Do you want a drink?'
'Are you studying or working?'

When we stopped dancing he . . . .

. . . .

. . . .

'Where are you staying?'
'Can I see you again?'
'Have you seen the new Michael Jackson film?'

Later he . . . .

. . . .

. . . .

5 Tell a story

a Form three or four groups. The teacher writes this sentence on the board: 'And that's why I can never forget the name Kathy.'

b The teacher then starts the story by saying, 'It was a dark and stormy night. Outside it was pouring with rain, and I was sitting alone in front of the fire. Suddenly I heard a scream . . .'

c The groups now continue the story in any way they like. One student at a time adds one sentence to the story until it finishes with the sentence on the board. A 'secretary' makes notes of the group's story. Each student thinks of three sentences.

d The secretary of each group tells the rest of the class the story his/her group thought of.

Grammar summary: page 83

1 🎧 Asking permission

A *Can I use the phone, please?*
B *Yes, of course. Go ahead.*

C *Is it OK if I leave early today? I'm going to the dentist's.*
D *Yes, that's fine.*

E *Would it be all right if I came home late tonight?*
F *Where are you going?*
E *To a party.*
F *Yes, OK. But don't be too late.*

G *Do you mind if I smoke?*
H *Well, I'd rather you didn't actually.*
G *Oh, sorry . . . OK.*

a Practise these dialogues in pairs. Change roles.

b Now imagine you're in the following situations. Improvise dialogues using the phrases on the right.

1 You're in a crowded cafe. There's a chair free but there are already two people sitting at that table. Ask permission to sit down.
2 You're living with an English family. You've got some friends up in your room. You want to make some coffee and take it up to them. Ask your landlady's permission.
3 You've just played tennis. You want to have a shower and then use your landlady's hairdryer.
4 You're at a station. Your train leaves in three minutes. There are two people in front of you in the queue at the ticket office. Ask permission to go to to the front of the queue.

Can
Could | I . . . ?
May

Is it
Would it be | all right if I . . . ?

Yes, | of course.
OK.
all right.
go ahead.

No, | I'm afraid . . .
I'm sorry . . .
I'd rather you didn't.

Do
Would | you mind if I . . .

No, not at all.
Well, actually . . .

2 Act it out

Work in pairs. Student A looks at the instructions on this page. Student B looks at the instructions on page 78.

Situation 1
You're living with an English family.

● You want to invite five or six friends home.
● You want to cook them something (one of your national dishes).
● You want to play them a few records which you've brought with you and maybe dance.
● You want to phone your friends to tell them what time to come.

Ask permission. Don't ask all the questions at once – be diplomatic.

Situation 2
You've got a foreign student staying with you. He/She's going to ask your permission to do various things.

● You've already prepared the evening meal, something special.
● You haven't got any bread.
● You worry if your student is out very late.
● You don't like being woken up late.
● Your bike has no lights on it.

Be friendly and helpful, not just negative.

3 What to say at mealtimes

A *Is that enough spaghetti for you, Luigi?*
B *Oh . . . Yes, thanks. That's fine.*
A *More meat sauce?*
B *Yes, please. Just a little.*
C *Would you like some ketchup on it?*
A *Um . . . No, thanks.*
C *What would you like to drink? Wine?*
B *No, thanks. Can I have a glass of water, please?*
C *Yes, of course. Help yourself.*

(later)

B *Can you pass the pepper, please?*
A *Yes, here you are.*

(later)

A *Would you like some more?*
B *Um . . . No, thanks. It was lovely but I'm full.*
A *Are you sure?*
B *Yes, quite sure. It was very nice. Thank you.*
A *How about some apple pie?*
B *Yes, please.*
C *Cream?*
B *No, thanks. I'm not too keen on cream.*

(later)

That was a lovely meal. Thank you very much.
A *I'm glad you enjoyed it.*
B *Is it all right if I go now? I'm meeting a friend at 8 o'clock.*
A *Yes, of course. Have a nice time.*

a Underline the phrases Luigi uses to speak politely.

b In pairs or groups improvise a dialogue based on the Sunday lunch in the picture.

4 Making offers

A *Shall I clear the table?*
B *No, that's OK. I'll do it.*
A *Well, would you like me to wash up then?*
B *No, it's OK, it all goes in the dishwasher.*
A *Let me make the coffee then.*
B *Yes, all right. That's nice of you.*

a Practise the dialogue in pairs.

b Now improvise similar dialogues for these situations.

1

2

5 Apologizing

Listen to four conversations on the cassette and write down what happened in each situation.

6 Bad news

Work in pairs. Student A looks at the information below. Student B looks at the information on page 79.

Your friend gave you £20 yesterday to buy him/her a ticket to a rock concert.

You completely forgot! By the time you remembered, all the tickets had been sold.

Break the news to your friend. Use any excuse(s) you can think of.

Apologize using these phrases.

I'm | very
terribly
really | sorry.

I'm afraid I've . . .

I feel | awful
terrible | about it.

I don't know what to say . . .

Summary of English in situations

- asking permission
- giving and refusing permission
- accepting and refusing food at mealtimes
- making offers
- apologizing and responding to apologies

21

1 🎧 Sound right

a Listen to the five words on the cassette. They all end in different long vowel sounds.

[iː]	[ɑː]	[uː]	[ɔː]	[ɜː]
see	car	you	for	her

b All the words in the box have a long vowel sound in the middle. Listen to them on the cassette and put them into the right column above.

> moon heart heard walk shirt
> laugh leave half lose piece nurse
> horse June caught meat

c In pairs, practise saying the words you have written in the columns. Then think of two words to add to each column.

2 🎧 Listen to this

Listen to a radio news bulletin on the cassette. It contains several mistakes. Make a note of the mistakes you hear. Compare your answers with your partner's. Listen again if you disagree.

3 Time to talk

A time capsule

You are going to put ten things into a 'time capsule'. The capsule will be buried, and then opened in 50 years' time.

The things you choose should show what life is like today.

Examples:
- today's newspaper
- photographs of current hairstyles
- the prices of a number of things.

a Working on your own, choose five things you would put into a time capsule.

b Form groups. Each person reads out his/her list. Discuss the lists and decide on the five things the group would put into the time capsule.

c The groups compare their lists. Discuss them, and make a final list of the five things the whole class agrees about.

4 Work on words

a Write each of the phrases below in the correct column.

make	do
	your homework

progress	a mess
your bed	your best
the ironing	exercise
a mistake	a job
something wrong	business
	a cake
the washing up	an exam
military service	a test
friends with someone	a profit
	a meal
the shopping	money
the housework	an exercise
a phone call	a suggestion
somebody a favour	

b Complete the following sentences using make or do in the correct tense

Example:
I hate . . . exams
I hate doing exams.

1 I always . . . the same mistake.
2 Can you . . . me a favour?
3 I'll . . . the dinner if you . . . the washing up.
4 I think we've already . . . this exercise.
5 My doctor advised me to . . . more exercise.
6 I'd like to . . . a collect call to Mexico, please.
7 Do you have to . . . military service in your country?
8 We are hoping to . . . business with several Japanese companies.

5 Language games

Get up and do it

a Form two teams, A and B.

b Each team looks at the following verbs and discusses what each one means.

c One member of team A demonstrates or mimes one of the verbs. Team B must guess what verb it is. Then a member of team B does the same with another verb, and so on. One point for each correct guess.

> shake hands
> shake your fist
> fold your arms
> rub your eyes
> snap your fingers
> shake your head
> shrug your shoulders
> put your hand up
>
> | | | |
> |---|---|---|
> | wave | clap | point |
> | salute | pinch | punch |
> | slap | scratch | hug |
> | squeeze | tickle | beckon |
> | stretch | nod | stroke |
>
> frown   wink
> blink   stare   glance

d 📺 Now listen to the cassette and follow the instructions.

6 Read and think

Read this paragraph very carefully.

> I want to know how quickly you can find out what is so odd and uncommon about this paragraph. You must work on your own - nobody can assist you, I'm afraid. You must try your skill at figuring out what is wrong, without talking to anybody. If you know what is wrong do not say anything - just wait for your companions to finish. At first sight it looks so ordinary that you may think that nothing is unusual about it at all. But as soon as you look at it word by word you will find out what is wrong with it. Work as quickly as you can. Good luck!

7 Now you're here

Buy a local newspaper and from it find out the answers to the following questions.

1 How much does it cost?
2 What's the weather forecast for tomorrow?
3 What will be on Channel 4 at 11 o'clock this evening?
4 What's the editorial about?
5 What's the name and frequency of the local BBC radio station?
6 What's the news in the Stop Press (Late News) column?
7 What's the name of the local ITV company?
8 What's a typical price for a 1987 Ford Escort?
9 What's the most popular boy's/girl's name in the Births Column?
10 What sort of wages are offered for: a) a cleaner b) a typist?
11 What's the horoscope for a Gemini?
12 Name two films which are on at local cinemas.

GRAMMAR IN ACTION

🖳 Food for thought

What do British people eat nowadays, and how well do they eat? A newspaper interviewed hundreds of people about what they ate.

Here are three people with very different diets.

Lee Harris (20)
vandriver

Amanda Page (19)
university student

Brian Watson (49)
insurance clerk

Do you eat between meals? If so, what and how much?

'Yes, a lot of crisps, salt and vinegar usually. Then I have a few biscuits and, sometimes a couple of Mars bars.'

'Just one or two apples or a yoghurt, but hardly any sweets. That's very little really, isn't it?'

'Yes, I treat myself to a doughnut with my morning coffee. And I suck a lot of Polos - a packet a day, at least.'

How much junk food do you eat?

'How much what? Oh yeah, well I eat what I like. I don't care what other people call it. I have plenty of chips, hamburgers, hot dogs . . . things like that. And I have an Indian takeaway once a week. But that isn't much, is it?'

'It depends on what you mean by junk food, doesn't it? I live on my own, so I eat a lot of convenience food, you know, frozen pizzas and quiches, and so on. But I don't eat any meat at all because I'm a vegetarian.'

'I have fish and chips from the local chip shop maybe once a week, but I wouldn't call that junk food, would you? I'm a "meat and two veg" man myself, I don't like fast food - I want to sit down at a table and have a proper meal.'

How healthy do you think your diet is?

'I don't know. I haven't thought about it. But I feel OK. I eat as much as I need. I have a few cans of lager every night but that's all right, isn't it?'

'I try to eat well. I eat plenty of high-fibre food, like wholemeal bread and fresh vegetables, and I don't eat much fatty food, and very little salt or sugar.'

'Quite healthy, I suppose. I've changed to Flora from butter, and I don't eat many eggs. As for alcohol, I only drink a little - about three or four pints of beer a week.'

1 Who eats what?

Read the text carefully and then write L (Lee), A (Amanda) or B (Brian) in the space provided.

1 Who eats the most sweets? . . .
2 Who has the healthiest diet? . . .
3 Who drinks the most alcohol? . . .
4 Who doesn't eat meat? . . .
5 Who only drinks beer? . . .
6 Who eats the most junk food? . . .
7 Who eats the most high-fibre food? . . .
8 Who eats chocolate? . . .
9 Who doesn't like 'fast' or convenience food? . . .
10 Who has margarine rather than butter? . . .

2 Grammar practice

Each of the sentences below can only be completed with three of the words or phrases. The other three are not possible. Tick (√) the correct alternatives.

1 He ate	a couple of a little of a few several much any	potatoes.

2 She had	a little a few very little much any hardly any	sugar in her coffee.

3 He doesn't drink	any some much hardly any many a lot of	alcohol.

4 He didn't eat	many much some a lot of any very little	sweets.

5 Does she eat	much many a few any some plenty of	bread?

3 What's missing?

Practise this dialogue in pairs, adding the question tags. Change roles.

A You don't eat meat, . . . ?
B No, I don't.
A So you're a vegetarian, . . . ?
B Yes, I am.
A But you eat fish, . . . ?
B Yes, I do.
A But eating fish is the same as eating meat, . . . ?
B Yes, I suppose it is.
A So you're not really a vegetarian, . . . ?
B It depends what you mean by 'vegetarian', . . . ?
A How do you mean?
B Well, vegetarians eat lots of vegetables, . . . ?
A Yes?
B But they don't eat red meat, . . . ?
A No.
B But they can choose whether or not to eat fish, . . . ?
A Yes, I suppose so.
B So I *am* a vegetarian, . . . ?

4 The future of food

There have been many changes in our eating habits over the last few years. Few people sit down to 'meat and two veg' each night. What will we eat in the future?

a Read what this food expert has to say about how our buying and eating habits will change in the future.

'I don't think there'll be ordinary cookers in the kitchens of the future. There'll only be microwaves and other new gadgets like that.
   We probably won't buy raw, unprepared ingredients. We'll simply choose pre-cooked meals from a huge selection of boxes on the shelf, like books in a library. And in time we won't even have to go down to the local supermarket to buy them. We'll bring up a menu on our TV screens and select three course meals from there. They'll then be delivered and all we'll have to do is heat them. Not everybody will like this convenience food but it'll give us a lot more free time - to go to restaurants to eat real food for example.'

b Work in pairs. Discuss the following:

● What sort of gadgets will kitchens of the future have / not have?
● How much cooking will people do?
● How will people do their food shopping?
● How will they use their free time?
● What other changes in our food production, buying and eating habits do you think there will be?

5 ▣ Making an omelette

Listen to the method for making an omelette. Put the instructions into the correct order from 1–7 and write in the missing verbs.

- [ ] . . . a little salt.
- [ ] . . . the omelette in half, and . . . it on to a hot dish.
- [ ] . . . the contents of the bowl into the frying pan and leave for a moment.
- [1] *Break* 5–6 eggs in a bowl.
- [ ] . . . butter or margarine in a frying pan until melted.
- [ ] . . . the edges of the omelette slightly, making the uncooked egg run under.
- [ ] . . . the eggs lightly.

Grammar summary: page 83

25

1 Describing where buildings/places are

a In pairs describe places on the map using the phrases in the box.

> on the right/left of   between
> on the corner of   opposite
> in front of   next to/beside
> near/by   at the end of   behind

b Now take turns at describing where the following are.

Town Hall	Post Office
Police Station	Travel Agent
Health Centre	Primary school
Multi-storey car park	Off licence

2 Where do they want to go?

a Which of the following can you find on the map?

> junction   fork   roundabout   crossroads   turning   footpath
> dual carriageway   zebra crossing   pedestrian crossing   flyover   bend
> one-way street   dead end

b 🖵 Listen to three conversations on the cassette. They all take place in the coach station. Follow the directions you hear and draw arrows (→ → →) on the map. Where does each person want to go?

> The first person wants to go to: ....
> The second person wants to go to: ....
> The third person wants to go to: ....

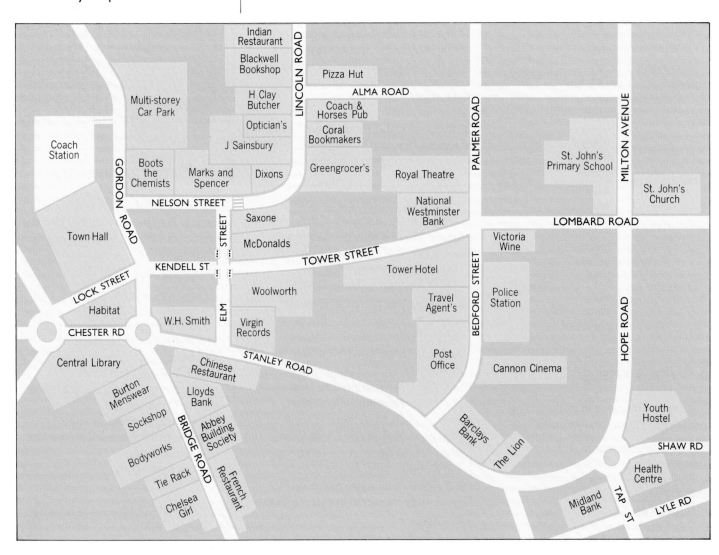

3 Asking for and giving directions

a Look at these phrases:

Can you tell me | where . . . is, please?
Do you know |

Can you tell me the way to . . . , please?

Thanks | very much.
| a lot.

Go | along | this street.
| up |
| down |

Go | past | . . .
| as far as |

Keep going until you come to . . .

Then take the | first |
| second |
| third |

turning on the | right.
| left.

Take the | left | fork.
| right |

You're welcome.
That's OK.
That's all right.

b Work in pairs. You are outside the Youth Hostel in Hope Road. Take it in turns to ask for and give directions to places on the map. Use the phrases above. Each student should ask for directions to three places.

4  In a bank

Listen to the following dialogues.

Changing money

A Can I change these German marks into pounds, please?
B Certainly. How many have you got?
A 200. What's the exchange rate today?
B 2.91 to the pound. How would you like the money?
A In fives, please.

Cashing traveller's cheques

A Hello. I'd like to cash these traveller's cheques, please.
B Yes. Have you got any identification?
A Yes, I've got my passport somewhere . . . Yes, here it is.
B Thank you. Can you write today's date and then just sign them, please?
A Here?
B Yes, that's right . . . How would you like the money?
A In tens and a few fives, please. Thank you.

In pairs practise your own dialogues for these situations using different currencies and amounts, etc.

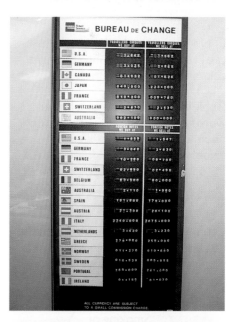

Summary of English in situations

- describing where buildings/ places are
- asking for and giving directions
- changing money
- cashing traveller's cheques

27

1 🔊 Sound right

a Put these words into the columns below according to their pronunciation:

noise   grey   care   noun
known   buy   near

Example:

[aɪ]	[eɪ]	[ɔɪ]	[aʊ]
try	day	boys	brown

[əʊ]	[ɪə]	[eə]
go	here	pair

b Listen and repeat the pairs of rhyming words.

c Now listen to the words on the cassette and put them into the right columns above.

d Now listen and repeat all three words in each column. Then think of two more words to go in each column.

2 🔊 Listen to this

Listen to some short questions on the cassette and write down where you would hear them. Choose from the places in the box.

Example:

Smoking or non–smoking?

an airport

a café	a pub
a theatre	a bank
a bookshop	an airport
a hot dog stand	a clothes shop
a railway station	a sandwich bar
a record shop	

3 Time to talk

Work in pairs or small groups. Read the following strange and amazing statements. Discuss whether you think they are true or false. If you think they are true, can you explain why? Compare your answers with other groups'.

1 There are only two words in the English language which end in the letters *shion*. They are *cushion* and *fashion*.

2 A fly born on a Sunday can be a grandfather by the following Wednesday.

3 The average person has fewer than two legs.

4 If you fly to New York on Concorde, you arrive two hours before your departure.

5 Large python snakes can swallow a whole pig and then eat nothing else for a year.

6 In nearly every language in the world, the word for *mother* begins with the 'm' sound.

7 The average human body contains about 90,000 kilometres of blood vessels.

8 The door to number 10 Downing Street, the Prime Minister's residence, can only be opened from the inside.

9 About a hundred people die every minute in the world but over two hundred are born.

4 Read and think

The woman who swallowed a mouse

Read the following sentences carefully and put them in the correct order to tell the story.

- [ ] a) 'I'll come as quickly as I can,' said the doctor. 'Listen carefully to my instructions.'
- [ ] b) 'You idiot!' shouted the doctor, 'I said a piece of CHEESE, not a piece of fish.'
- [1] c) One morning, a man phoned the doctor. He was almost hysterical.
- [ ] d) 'Then make your wife open her mouth and hold the cheese above her face.'
- [ ] e) As soon as the doctor arrived at the house he rushed in through the open front door.
- [ ] f) 'Don't panic. Keep calm. First, go to the front door and leave it open.'
- [ ] g) 'Hold the cheese in that position till I arrive.'
- [ ] h) 'When you've done that go quickly to the fridge and get a piece of cheese.'
- [ ] i) He found the man holding a fish's head above his wife's open mouth.
- [ ] j) 'Please come quickly, doctor, my wife has swallowed a mouse.'
- [ ] k) 'Tie the piece of cheese to a piece of string.'
- [ ] l) 'No, you don't understand, doctor,' said the man. 'I've got to get the cat out first.'

5 Work on words

a Work in pairs. Complete the following dialogue with adjectives from the box below. Use each of them only once.

A What was Pete's party like?
B It was . . .
A What about the music?
B It was . . . – I couldn't hear myself speak.
A Did you eat anything?
B No – I was . . . but the food was . . . , so I didn't eat a thing.
A Were there many people there?
B Yes – hundreds. The flat was . . . , so it was . . . and . . . hot.
A What time did it finish?
B At about 1.30. A person in the flat above complained about the noise – he was . . . He was a . . . man, and I was . . . he would hit Pete.
A Were you . . . ?
B Yes, I was a bit.
A What time did you get home?
B I had to walk home because there were no taxis. It was snowing, and I was . . . By the time I got home I was completely . . .
A What are you doing today?
B I'm going round to Pete's to help clear up. I'm sure the flat's . . .
A I'm . . . – you never clear this flat up.

packed	starving	furious
amazed	tiny	filthy
positive	huge	terrified
exhausted	awful	boiling
great	freezing	deafening

b Act out the dialogues. Think carefully about the words you've written in. They carry a lot of meaning and may need to be stressed.

6 Language games

Think before you speak

a Form two teams, A and B.

b A student from Team A comes out in front of the class. Team B have a minute to ask him/her questions. The student must answer quickly but is not allowed to say 'yes' or 'no'. Team A win a point if their student survives for a minute.

Example:
Team B *Your name is Alain, isn't it?*
Student A *That's right.*
Team B *And you're French?*
Student A *I am.*
Team B *When did you arrive?*
Student A *Last week.*
Team B *Last month?*
Student A *I said 'last week'.*

c Now a student from Team B comes out to the front of the class to be questioned.

d You can also play the game in pairs or small groups.

7 Now you're here

Many people, before they visit Britain for the first time, have certain ideas about what British people are like. These ideas, or stereotypes, may or may not be true.

a Work in pairs or groups. Read these questions and decide how you think a typical British person would answer them.

1 Do you own a bowler hat? (How often do you wear it?)

2 Do you always have tea at 5 o'clock?

3 Do you normally have a cooked English breakfast?

4 Do you know the rules of cricket?

5 How often do you have roast beef and Yorkshire pudding for lunch on Sunday?

b Now write five more questions on what you've heard or been told about Britain and the British.

c Find out how true these stereotypes of British people are. Ask two or more British people the ten questions and then compare your answers in class the next day.

UNIT FIVE

LESSON ONE

Our Picture of Britain

We are two French students staying in England, and we wonder why the British are so obsessed with television. We see people watching TV all day, even during meals and when they have guests. The TV is also left on when no one is watching it. You seem to prefer to watch TV rather than talk to each other. Are we wrong?

Michelle Verrier and **Danielle Richard**
Bournemouth

I What do you think?

a Before reading the text on the right, read through the following statements. Do you think they are true or not? Mark them with a tick (√) or a cross (×).

1 People who live on their own watch more television than people who live in a family.
2 Soap operas are the most popular programmes on British television.
3 More men watch soap operas than women.
4 Most British soap operas are about rich, good-looking people.
5 Violent programmes are only shown after midnight.
6 It's usually the man in the house who decides what programmes to watch.
7 More than half the viewers in Britain think there is too much sport on TV.
8 Commercials are more popular with young people than with their parents.

b Now read the text and see how many answers you got right.

The British obsession?

A member of an average British family watches 22 hours of television a week. A person living alone watches even more than that — 36 hours.

Soap operas are by far the most popular programmes on British TV. They are more popular with women than men. However, it is estimated that one in eight people watch soap operas in secret (most of them are men).

British soap operas are more realistic and less glamorous than American ones. American 'soaps' portray good-looking, successful, and super-rich people. In contrast, people in British soaps are much poorer, more ordinary and less attractive.

On British TV, there is a rule that the most violent programmes can only be shown after nine o'clock. In fact opinion polls indicate that viewers would prefer to see less violence on TV altogether.

The most common reason given by young people under 20 for watching television (two thirds, in fact) is, that it gives them something to do.

It is twice as likely to be the woman in the house rather than the man who controls which channel they watch.

A third of viewers said they would prefer to see fewer programmes on sport — two thirds of these were female.

The attitude of many young people towards commercials on TV is 'the more the better'. 38% are in favour of more rather than fewer commercials and a quarter of young people would rather watch the commercials than the programmes (because they think they are better). More than 50% of them stay to watch the ads during the commercial breaks as compared to fewer than 30% of adults.

With the coming of satellite and cable TV, the choice of channels and programmes is becoming wider and wider. But over a third of British people think that the more programmes there are, the worse they will be and over a half say they would rather have a choice of only four channels.

2 Grammar practice

a Choose words to complete these sentences with a comparative or a superlative.

Example:
Soap operas . . . game shows.
Soap operas are more popular than game shows.

Late night programmes are often . . .
Late night programmes are often the best.

1 With satellite TV, viewers have a . . . choice but the programmes may be . . .
2 The . . . programmes are not necessarily the . . .
3 Many young people are . . . in the commercials because they are . . . than the programmes they interrupt.
4 We only see the . . . American programmes in this country. It's difficult to imagine what the . . . are like.

b Now write complete sentences as in this example:

Videos are becoming (cheap).
Videos are becoming cheaper and cheaper.

5 Some people think the quality of programmes is becoming (bad).
6 Videos are becoming (complicated).
7 With modern TV sets the picture quality is getting (good).
8 There are (many) channels to choose from nowadays.

3 🎧 What's the product?

Listen to the advertisements on the cassette and write down what type of products you think they are advertising.

Example:
1 *camera film*

4 Make comparisons

a Compare British television and television in your country. Write a sentence about each of the aspects below.

Example:
Commercials are much more frequent on Spanish than on British television.

1 the quality of the commercials
2 the frequency of commercial breaks
3 the realism of the soap operas
4 the degree of violence
5 the number of channels
6 the number of imported American programmes
7 the number of sports programmes
8 any other aspect of television

b Compare your sentences with those of other students. Have they made similar comparisons?

5 What would you prefer?

a Work in pairs. Ask each other questions using *Would you rather . . . ?* or *Would you prefer to . . . ?*

Example:
A *Would you rather watch TV or go out for a coffee?*
B *I'd rather go out for a coffee.*
A *Why?*
B *Because it's more fun talking to people than watching TV.*

1 watch TV / go out?
2 be an only child / have a lot of brothers and sisters?
3 have an interesting job that's badly paid / have a boring job that's very well paid?
4 live in a city / live in the countryside?
5 be famous / be unknown?
6 be a boy / be a girl?
7 live a short but rich life / have a long but poor life?
8 get married at 20 / get married at 30?
9 give a present / receive a present?

b Think of three similar questions to ask each other in the same way.

6 Britain and your country

a Write sentences comparing Britain and your country in at least five ways suggested by the photos below.

b Read out what you have written. Discuss the differences.

Grammar summary: page 84

31

1 ▥ Talking on the phone

A *Hello? 462200.*
B *Hello. Can I speak to Lewis, please?*
A *Lewis? I'm sorry, I think you've got the wrong number.*
B *Is that 472200?*
A *No, it's 462200.*
B *Oh, I'm sorry. It __is__ the wrong number. Sorry to bother you.*
A *That's OK. Goodbye.*

C *857 0099.*
D *Hello. Could I speak to Kim, please?*
C *Speaking.*
D *Oh, hi Kim. This is Rob. Um . . . What are you doing tonight?*

E *Hello?*
F *Hello, this is Andy. Is Kathy there, please?*
E *I'm not sure. Can you hang on a moment?*

   (pause)

   Hello? No, I'm afraid she's not in. Can I take a message?
F *Yes. Can you ask her to phone Andy as soon as possible? My number's 3-6-4-2-1-7.*
E *3-6-4-2-1-7. Yeah, I've got that. I'll give her the message.*
F *Thanks a lot. Bye bye, then.*

a Practise the three dialogues in pairs, using your own names.

b Act out similar conversations without looking in your books.

2 ▥ Can I take a message?

Listen to two telephone conversations and write down the messages.

MESSAGES

MESSAGES

3 Making phone calls

Work in pairs. Student A reads the instructions on this page. Student B looks at the instructions on page 79.

Situation 1

Phone your friend Chris. If he/she is not in leave a message. You want to tell him/her that the party is at the Sagittarius Club in Berwick Street. You want to meet Chris in a pub called the Fortescue in Marylebone Road at 9.50 p.m. If there's any problem he/she can ring you. Your number is 865 2443.

Situation 2

Phone your friend Alex. You've lost your address book and you're supposed to be meeting a friend, Sam, tonight at his house. If Alex is in, find out:

● Sam's second name
● Sam's address
● Sam's phone number.

Make sure you spell everything correctly.

4 📺 Make a call

A *Hello. Can you get me the International Operator, please?*
B *Is that a general enquiry or a directory enquiry?*
A *A general enquiry.*
B *The number's 155.*
A *Thank you.*

(pause)

Hello. Is that International?
C *It is. Can I help you?*
A *Yes, I was speaking to a number in Brazil. The line was very bad and then we were cut off. Could you try to get me a better line, please?*
C *I'll do my best. What number is it?*
A *010 55 81 755308.*
C *Right. Hold the line, caller. I'll try it for you.*

(pause)

I'm sorry, I'm getting an engaged tone. What's your number, please?
A *01 327 8899.*
C *Right. Replace your receiver and I'll call you back.*

a Practise the dialogue in pairs.

b Now improvise phone conversations for these situations.

1 Ring the operator and ask what time it is in your country and then tell him/her you want to make a 'reverse charge' (or 'collect') call to a friend in your country.

2 Ring your host family and tell them that you aren't coming home for dinner tonight.

3 Find out the number of the Youth Hostel in Bath from Directory Enquiries. Book a bed for two nights next weekend and ask about the price.

4 Ring the police. You've lost your bag. Describe it and ask them if anybody has taken it to the police station.

5 Ring the Sports Centre and book a squash court for this evening, between 8 and 9p.m.

6 Ring a friend who's staying with a British family. He/She isn't in, so you have to leave a message. You can't meet him/her until 9.30 this evening.

7 Ring the operator and tell him/her you want an alarm call at a certain time early tomorrow morning.

Summary of English in situations

- using the telephone
- taking and leaving telephone messages
- spelling in English

1 🎧 Sound right

a You will hear these pairs of words on the cassette. Listen carefully to the sounds they start with.

west	vest	they	day
red	led	ship	chip
ban	van	I	high
dry	try	pat	bat
thin	tin	jet	yet

What's the difference in the pronunciation of the words in each pair?

b Now listen and repeat the pairs of words.

c Choose six of the words above and put them in squares like this.

west	pat	high
ban	they	yet

You must not choose both words from a pair.

Example:
not *west* and *vest*.

d Your teacher will now read out words from a) above. Cross out your words as you hear them. When all of your words are crossed out, shout BINGO!

2 🎧 Listen to this

Listen to ten jokes on the cassette. The punch-line for each one is missing. In pairs or groups retell the jokes and decide on suitable punch-lines. Compare your ideas with the complete jokes on the cassette.

3 Language games

How many words?

Form two to four teams and make as many words as you can from the word:

ENTERTAINMENT

The words must have three letters or more. You must know what the words mean. You must *not* use dictionaries.

You score one point for each word on your list. You get an extra point for every word with five letters or more.

You get an extra point if you have a word on your list which the other team(s) haven't got. The team with the most points is the winner.

TRAIN

EAT

TAME

4 Time to talk

The world needs me!

a Five students come to the front of the class. They must imagine they are travelling in a hot air balloon. Each one chooses to be a famous person, living or dead.

b There is very little food and water left in the balloon, and the only way to save any lives is to throw people out, one at a time. Each person in the balloon explains to the class why he/ she should be saved.

c The class discuss the travellers' arguments and vote on who should be thrown out first, second, third and fourth. The person who is saved is the winner.

5 Read and think

Read the following instructions carefully and follow them exactly. You need a large piece of blank paper and a pen. You are going to draw something without taking your pen off the paper until you have finished following all the instructions.

Near the top of the paper draw a large number six. When you finish the circle of the six, draw a line diagonally down to the left, and now draw the number four under the six. At the bottom of the number four draw an inverted C (a C drawn the opposite way to usual). Now draw a vertical line down from the bottom of the inverted C (about one centimetre long) and then join that line to the top of the six by drawing a large inverted C. Midway along the large inverted C, on the inside (opposite the four), draw an oval (like an egg standing vertically). Finally, take your pen off the paper and draw a round black circle in the middle of the circle of the six.

Now compare your drawing with your partner's.

6 Work on words

a Put the adjectives on the right into three columns according to whether they are positive, negative or either.

Positive	Negative	Either positive or negative

b Decide which four positive adjectives and which four negative adjectives best describe you.

c Go round the class finding other students with the same star sign as yourself. Compare your lists of adjectives. How similar are your personalities? The star signs are:

independent loyal humble
sentimental reserved indecisive
selfish adventurous brave
impulsive aggressive determined
patient possessive stubborn
practical artistic moody
talkative sensitive superficial
lively imaginative shy
quick–tempered generous
big–headed snobbish ambitious
vain modest hard–working
organized fussy charming
flirtatious romantic idealistic
unreliable jealous intense
energetic optimistic
irresponsible tactless frank
careless mean pessimistic
sensible

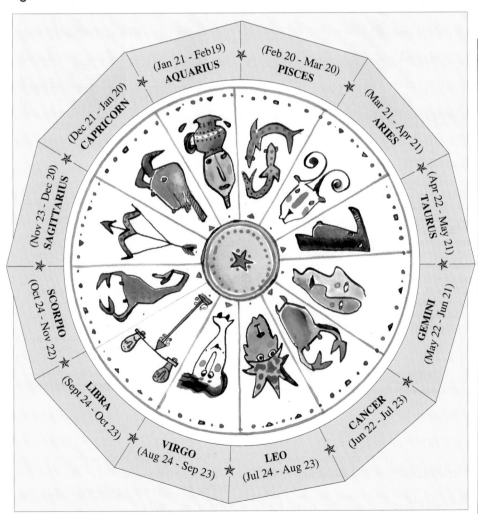

d Now list the most common adjectives for each star sign and write a short description of a typical personality for each one.

7 Now you're here

Ask a British person the following questions.

1 Do you rent or own your television?
2 How much is the television licence fee at the moment? (Black and white? Colour? Why do you have to have a licence? What happens if you haven't got one?)
3 Do you have to have a licence for a radio or video?
4 How many different channels can you watch?
5 Are there enough television channels?
6 Which channel do you watch the most/least?
7 What's your favourite/least favourite programme?
8 Do you watch soap operas? (Which ones?)
9 Who's your least favourite television personality?
10 How many commercial breaks are there per hour on commercial television?
11 Are there too many/few American programmes on British TV?
12 Do you think there's too much violence on TV?

GRAMMAR IN ACTION

📷 Bird's-eye view of London

St Paul's Cathedral

St Paul's Cathedral was built between 1675 and 1710. For one of the best views of London you must climb 650 steps up to the Golden Gallery at the very top, where you're 111 metres above the ground.

Cristina Garcia from Valencia has stopped after only 259 steps, at the Whispering Gallery.

'I've just sent my sister round to the other side of the dome, 30 metres away. When she whispers something to me, I'll be able to hear it if I put my ear close to the wall.'

'Have you been up to the top yet?'

'No, I've already climbed enough steps for one day!'

Tower Bridge

Tower Bridge was opened in 1894. It is 244 metres long and 100 metres high. Enough bricks were used in its construction to build 350 houses.

'Before I came here, I thought Tower Bridge was the same as London Bridge,' said Pascal Bouchet from Toulouse. 'But now I've seen London Bridge from the top of Tower Bridge, so I know they're different. But I'm a bit disappointed - I've been waiting here since eleven o'clock this morning, and the bridge hasn't opened yet. I'm freezing!'

The Monument

The Monument is a tall, hollow column with a golden ball at the top. It is 70 metres high. It was designed in 1671 and completed in 1677. It commemorates the Great Fire of London in 1666, in which most of the city was burnt down. The fire started in a baker's shop in Pudding Lane nearby. Maki Onuma has just climbed the 311 steps to the top.

'I'm exhausted, I've been standing here for ten minutes now, just looking at the view. From here you can see the Tower of London, Big Ben and The Post Office Tower. It's amazing! I've brought my video camera with me to make a film of it all!'

1 Right or wrong?

Mark these sentences right (√) or wrong (×).

1 St Paul's Cathedral was built in the sixteenth century.
2 The Whispering Gallery is higher than the Golden Gallery.
3 You can whisper to somebody 30 metres away inside the dome of St. Paul's.
4 Tower Bridge is another name for London Bridge.
5 Tower Bridge is 200 years old.
6 The bridge was built with the bricks from 350 houses.
7 The Monument has fewer steps than St. Paul's.
8 The Great Fire of London started exactly where the Monument stands.

2 Grammar practice

a Choose verbs to complete the following sentences using the past simple or the present perfect tense (simple or continuous).

Example:
. . . the film last night?
Did you see the film last night?

1 How long . . . in England?
Three months. I . . . in April.
2 I . . . this book for two days now and . . . almost half of it.
3 How long . . . each other?
We . . . at school together, so that means I . . . Sammy for ten years.
4 I (not) . . . Laura for ages. She . . . very hard recently, and she (not) . . . time to see me.
5 What time . . . this morning?
I . . . at 6.00.

3 What's missing?

Complete the following sentences with *for*, *since*, *yet*, *just*, *already*, or *ago*. Use each preposition once.

1 I've been waiting here . . . five o'clock.
2 The film hasn't started . . .
3 They arrived twenty minutes . . .
4 Luke's happy. He's . . . had a letter from his girlfriend.
5 We've lived in this house . . . thirty years.
6 No, thanks. I've . . . seen that film four times.

4 Say it another way

Change the sentences from the past simple to the present perfect (simple or continuous).

Example:
I began to smoke when I was 14.

I've been smoking since I was 14.

1 I came to England two weeks ago.
I . . .
2 It started raining an hour ago.
I . . .
3 I bought this car a year ago.
I . . .
4 She first went to yoga classes last December.
She . . .
5 He first learnt to drive when he was seventeen.
He . . .
6 They got married in 1986.
They . . .

5 How long?

a Write down:

- the name of your oldest friend
- the name of the town / city you live in
- something you study apart from English
- your favourite sport or hobby
- the make of your or your parents' car
- your favourite possession.

b Show your partner your list and ask each other questions about what you've written. Write down the answers.

Example:
A *How long have known Giorgio?*
B *I've known him for about eight years.*

6 Quick questions

Have you ever . . . ?

a Move around the class asking questions to find one person who has done each of the things below. Remember to change the verb in brackets when you ask the questions. When you find a person who answers 'Yes, I have.' write down their first name and then ask them another question about the event.

Example:
Student A *Have you ever won a lottery or competition?*
Student B *Yes, I have.*
Student A *How much money did you win?*
Student B *250 francs.*

(win) a competition or cup
(meet) anybody famous
(be) in the papers / on television
(read) a novel in English
(eat) snails or frogs' legs
(hitch-hike)
(be) questioned by the police
(break) an arm or leg
(lose) consciousness
(be) attacked by an animal
(do) anything very dangerous
(fall) madly in love
(have) a car accident
(run) a marathon
(spend) more than a week in hospital
(write) poetry
(listen) to the BBC World Service

b When everyone's list is complete the class ask each other more questions about each of their experiences.

Example:
What did you do with the money?

7 ▣ What's just happened?

Listen to the voices and sounds on the cassette and say what has just happened.

Example:
The boy has just broken the window with a football.

Grammar summary: page 84

37

1 What are they wearing?

1	2	3

Describe what the people in this picture are wearing. Use the words in the box to help you.

tights   bracelet   zip   flat   patterned   leather   jeans   low-heeled ear-ring   long-sleeved   dark/light   blue   jacket   shoes   turn–ups denim   short-sleeved   check   skirt   dark glasses   T–shirt   shirt   no collar trousers   boots   striped   plain   chain necklace   blouse   pocket

2 The things you wear

a Do you know what all these items of clothing and accessories are?

a digital watch	a peaked cap
a mini-skirt	gloves
high-heeled shoes	knickers
lipstick	stockings
a suit	a cardigan
a bow tie	pyjamas
braces	a bikini
a bra	a jacket
aftershave	a blouse
a silk scarf	a silver ring
shorts	trainers
a tracksuit	a belt
sandals	pants
a vest	a swimsuit
perfume	

b Put the items into the three columns below, according to whether:

A you are wearing them now
B you wear them sometimes but not now
C you never wear them.

A	B	C

c Add three more items to each column.

3 ⊟ Shopping for clothes

A Can I help you?
B No, I'm just looking, thanks.

(later)

   Excuse me. Have you got this sweater in any other colours?
A What colour are you looking for?
B Yellow.
A Just a moment, I'll have a look. What size are you?
B Size 12, I think.
A Yes, here we are.
B That's a bit dark. Have you got a lighter shade than that?
A No, I'm afraid not.
B I think I'll leave it, thanks. It's not quite what I'm looking for.

(later)

   Are these jeans in the sale, too?
A Yes, they're half price.
B Can I try them on, please?
A Yes, of course, the changing room's over there.

(later)

B Yes, these fit me, I think.
A Oh, yes, and they really suit you. They look great.
B Yes, I'll have them. How much are they?
A £17. Are you paying cash or by credit card?
B Cash.

a Practise the dialogue in pairs. Change roles.

b Now improvise similar dialogues using different clothes, colours and sizes.

4 What's wrong?

Look at the picture on the right of models at a fashion show and listen to the commentary. Note down the mistakes you hear.

Example:
Alan's wearing a grey pin-stripe suit, not a dark blue checked suit.

5 Making a complaint

A *Excuse me. Um, I bought this T–shirt here yesterday. I took it home and then found it had a small hole by the sleeve – here. Could I change it, please?*
B *Oh dear . . . Yes, I see. Have you got the receipt?*
A *Yes, I have, luckily. Here it is.*
B *Well, if you'd like to change it, find another one on the rail.*
A *I don't think there are any left in my size. I've already looked.*
B *Well, in that case you can either have a refund or I can give you a credit note for the full amount.*
A *I think I'll have my money back then, please.*
B *There we are, £6.95. I'm sorry about that.*

Practise the dialogue in pairs. Change roles.

Stephanie
Alan
Joe

6 Act it out

Work in pairs. Student A reads the instructions below and Student B reads the instructions on page 79.

Situation 1

You bought a sweater from this shop two days ago. The assistant told you that it would stretch when you washed it. You washed it – it shrank! Talk to the manager about it. You speak first.

Situation 2

You are a shop assistant. You get commission on everything you sell. It's especially good on sweaters! Try to sell one to the next customer.

> **Summary of English in situations**
>
> - buying clothes
> - talking about sizes and colours
> - making complaints

1 🎧 Sound right

a Read through the following two syllable words. Underline the syllable which you think is stressed.

Example: <u>stu</u>dent

teacher	complain
arrive	either
effort	London

b Listen and check your answers.

c Listen again and repeat the words. Notice that the unstressed syllable has the sound [ə] as in 'the'. Circle those syllables.

Example: student

d Listen to eight two-syllable words on the cassette. Write them in the correct column below. There are two examples first.

Stress on first syllable	Stress on second syllable
doctor	complain

e Now circle the [ə] sound in each word.

Examples:

doctor   complain

f Listen and repeat the words. Remember to put a heavy stress on the stressed syllable.

2 Language games

In the manner of the word

One student (A) goes out of the classroom. The other students choose an adverb, for example, angrily. Student A comes back into the classroom. He/She has to guess what the adverb is by asking students to mime or do something 'in the manner of the word'.

Example:
Student A *Helga, say hello to Ali in the manner of the word.*

Student A has three guesses at the adverb.

3 🎧 Listen to this

Who's bluffing?

This is a radio programme in which one team defines a word in three different ways and the other team have to guess which is the correct definition.

a Listen to the definitions of words on the cassette and make notes.

b Work in pairs or groups. Discuss the definitions and decide which you think are the correct ones.

c Listen to the cassette to check your answers.

4 Time to talk

It is the year 2250. You have been chosen to be one of the citizens of a new city, Utopia. It is going to be a perfect society. Below are some of the proposed laws for Utopia.

a Read the proposed laws and decide whether you are for or against each one.

b Form groups. Debate the laws one by one, letting each member of the group say whether he/she is for or against it and why. Decide which laws you are going to impose.

1 Everybody should earn the same whatever their job.
2 Police officers should not carry guns.
3 Everybody should do military service for one year when they are 18.
4 Smoking ought not to be allowed on Utopia.
5 You should not be allowed to leave money to your relatives or children when you die.
6 There should only be one child per family.

c Each member of the group thinks of another law he/she wants to impose. Debate these new laws and add the ones you agree on to the list.

d Compare your final list of laws with other groups'.

5 Read and think

Combine phrases from the two columns to make examples of British graffiti ('writing on walls').

Example: 1 – j
Always be sincere – even when you don't mean it!

1 Always be sincere
2 I used to be big-headed.
3 Don't hate yourself in the morning.
4 Things are never as bad as they seem.
5 Laugh and the world laughs with you.
6 Don't panic – count to ten.
7 Stop air pollution.
8 Save water.
9 Don't shoot!
10 I was born this way.
11 Is there intelligent life on earth?
12 Nostalgia isn't what it used to be.

a) Sleep till noon.
b) Then panic.
c) Snore and you sleep alone!
d) Bath with a friend.
e) Yes, but I'm only visiting.
f) What's your excuse?
g) Quit breathing!
h) I don't want to be president.
i) True. It's a thing of the past.
j) even when you don't mean it!
k) Now I'm absolutely perfect.
l) No, they're much, much worse!

6 Work on words

a In pairs work out what these phrases and idioms mean.

Well done!	Watch out!	Cheers!
Take it easy.	Touch wood!	Cheer up!
Keep in touch.	It's up to you.	Say cheese.
Never mind.	I'm positive.	After you.
You're welcome.	Best of luck!	Sure, go ahead.
Come off it.	Get lost!	I don't mind.
I must be off.	Keep the change.	Make yourself at home.
Sweet dreams.	Bless you!	Keep your fingers crossed.
		Say when.

b Decide in which situation you might say them, and what the person you were talking to might say (or might have said).

c Write two short dialogues which include four of the phrases/idioms.

d Read or act out your dialogues.

7 Now you're here

a Answer the following questions about the home of the British family you're living with (or any British family you know).

1 Is it a house or a flat?
2 Is the area urban, suburban or rural?
3 If it's a house, what kind of house is it?
4 If it's a house, has it got a name? (Why is it called that?)
5 Which of the following rooms has it got?
  a) a dining room
  b) a study
  c) a basement
  d) an attic
  e) a spare bedroom
6 Is there a shower in the bathroom?
7 What do they call the sitting room?
8 What do they call the toilet?
9 Has it got double glazing?
10 Has it got central heating?
11 Has it got a garden? Describe it.
12 Has it got a garage?

b In what ways are British houses/flats different from those in your country?

c Compare your answers in class next day.

GRAMMAR IN ACTION

A . . . it was late at night and your car skidded off the road into a river and began sinking fast, upside down?

B . . . you were in the middle of a large field when you suddenly saw an angry bull coming towards you?

Are you a survivor?

What would you do if . . .

C . . . you were trapped by fire in an upstairs bedroom in a house?

D . . . you were driving at 100 kph downhill and your brakes failed?

E . . . you were cooking chips and the pan suddenly caught fire?

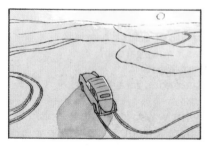

F . . . you ran out of petrol crossing a desert by car, alone, and you had very little water and no idea where you were?

G . . . you picked up a hitch-hiker in your car and he/she took out a knife and told you to drive to a place 100 kilometres away?

H . . . you were walking in a forest and the person you were with was bitten in the leg by a snake?

1 What was the question?

Here are some people's first reactions to the situations above. Match each answer to the appropriate situation.

Example: 1 – E

1 I'd throw it into the sink.
2 I'd try to open one of the doors.
3 I wouldn't go too far away from the car.
4 I'd try to signal to someone with my lights.
5 I'd tie a handkerchief over my mouth and nose.
6 First, I'd tie a handkerchief very tightly around it.
7 I'd sound the horn to warn other drivers to get out of the way.
8 I wouldn't run. I'd start walking backwards very slowly.

2 What would you do?

a Write down what you would do in each situation.

b Form groups, discuss and write down:
● what you think would be the best thing(s) to do in situations A–H.
● what you think you shouldn't do.

c Each group then tells the class their opinions.

3  Speaking of survival

You are going to hear some extracts from a radio programme on survival. Listen to the street interviews and write down which situation (A–H) each speaker is talking about.

1 E   5 . . .
2 . . .   6 . . .
3 . . .   7 . . .
4 . . .   8 . . .

4 Grammar practice

a Find verbs to complete the following questions. Think carefully about the tense of each verb.

Example:
What . . . if your car suddenly . . . on a level crossing?

What would you do if your car suddenly broke down on a level crossing?

1 . . . what to do if somebody . . . a heart attack?
2 If you . . . a person who you . . . had taken too many aspirins, how . . . them?
3 If the car in front of you . . . and . . . fire, how . . . rescue the people who were trapped inside?
4 How . . . if you . . . a mugger rob someone in the street?

b In pairs ask and answer the questions.

5 Consequences

Form groups of about four students. The teacher reads out a sentence beginning 'What would happen if . . . ?' The groups think of as many possible consequences as they can in one minute, and write them down. They compare lists. Score one point for each consequence no other group has thought of.

Example:
Teacher *What would happen if your face turned blue when you told a lie?*
Group 1 *Everyone would be completely honest.*
Group 2 *We'd all wear blue face make-up so no one would know when we lied.*

6 Telepathy

a Form two or three teams. One member of each team sits at the front of the class with his/her back to the team. Team members take it in turns to be the team 'leader'.

b Each team leader writes an ending to the first of the unfinished sentences below. The + or − indicates if the ending has to be positive or negative.

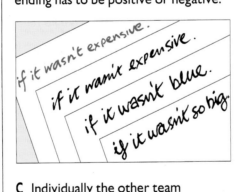

if it wasn't expensive.
if it wasn't expensive.
if it wasn't blue.
if it wasn't so big.

c Individually the other team members try to guess what their leader has written and write down the same ending to the sentence (without speaking to or copying from their team mates).

d The teams score one point for every student who guessed what their leader wrote.

1 I'd buy it if it . . . (−)
2 If it wasn't raining, we . . . (+)
3 I'd lend you my car if I . . . (−)
4 If we knew her number, we . . . (+)

7 What are you really like?

a Work in pairs. Student A asks B the questions and notes down his/her answers. Change roles.

Example:
Student A *If you were an animal, which animal would you choose to be?*
Student B *A lion.*

b Look at the key on page 79 and see what your answers tell you about yourself.

1 If (you/be) an animal, which animal (you/choose) to be?
  a) a horse
  b) a bird
  c) a sheep
  d) a lion
2 If (you/buy) a car, which colour (it/be)?
  a) black
  b) red
  c) green
  d) blue
3 If (you/win) £100,000 on a lottery, what (you/do) with it?
  a) buy a house
  b) go on a trip round the world
  c) share it with your family and friends
  d) put it in the bank
4 If (you/have) to choose only one of these, which (you/choose)?
  a) a long life
  b) fame
  c) a successful marriage
  d) wealth
5 If (you/be) a room in a house, which room do you think (you/be)?
  a) a kitchen
  b) a bedroom
  c) a bathroom
  d) a study
6 If (you/can) choose one of these jobs, which it (be)?
  a) a teacher
  b) an actor/actress
  c) a nurse
  d) a salesperson

Grammar summary: page 85

1 📺 Booking into a youth hostel

A *Hello. Have you got any beds left, please?*
B *Yes, I think we have. For how many people?*
A *Two – one boy and one girl.*
B *Yes, that's all right. Are you members?*
A *I am, but I'm afraid my girlfriend isn't.*
B *That's all right. She can have an International Guest Membership card. It isn't expensive. How long do you want to stay for?*
A *Just one night.*
B *You understand you can't share the same room.*
A *Yes, of course. How many beds are there in each room?*
B *Four.*
A *And do we have to do any jobs?*
B *Yes, you're expected to help with a bit of the cleaning and tidying of the hostel, but it'll only take you ten minutes or so.*
A *Can we eat here?*
B *Yes, we provide an evening meal or you can cook for yourself in the members' kitchen. It's the same for breakfast. But both meals are very cheap.*
A *We're a bit short of money. I think we'll cook our own, thanks. Do we have to pay extra for hot showers?*
B *No, baths and showers are included in the price. But you have to pay for the hire of a sheet sleeping bag.*
A *So how much will that be altogether?*
B *That'll be £18.60 excluding meals.*
A *OK, fine. Thanks very much.*

a Listen to the dialogue on the cassette.

b Act out similar conversations in which:

1 Two girls book in together. They are both members of the YHA. They want an evening meal but not breakfast. They've got their own sheet sleeping bags.
2 A boy books in. He is not a member. He wants to cook his own evening meal but have the hostel breakfast. He has his own sleeping bag but it is not cotton, as required.

2 📺 Booking into a B & B

A *Good evening. We'd like a room, please. Have you got any left?*
B *Yes, I've just got one left. Would you like to see it?*
A *Yes, please.*

   (later)

   Yes, that'll do fine. How much is it?
B *Bed and breakfast is £15.50 each.*
A *What time's breakfast?*
B *Between 7.30 and 9 o'clock. Would you like a cooked breakfast?*
A *Yes, please.*
B *If you're coming in late, I can lend you a front door key.*
A *Fine, thanks very much.*

a Practise the dialogue in pairs.

b Improvise similar dialogues in which you ask for:

1 a single room for two nights with continental breakfast.
2 a twin room (a room with two single beds) for one night with an evening meal and an early breakfast (7 o'clock).

3 Make up your minds

a Form groups of four (A, B, C and D). You are students at a language school in London and you've decided to go to Scotland for the weekend. You haven't decided how to get there. Student A's instructions are on page 78, B's are on page 79, C's on page 80 and D's on page 81. All students read their instructions.

b Discuss your travel arrangements. Use the phrases below to persuade your friends that your solution is the best. You must come to a decision.

I think we | *should*
ought to | *. . .*

It'd be (much) better to . . .
We could . . .
Why don't we . . .

How
What | *about . . . ?*

I see what you mean but . . .
That's true but . . .
I'm not so sure . . .

4 🖭 Buying a train ticket

A *Can I have a ticket to London, please?*
B *Second class?*
A *Yes, please.*
B *Single or return?*
A *Return, please.*
B *Are you coming back today?*
A *Yes, this evening.*
B *If you wait 20 minutes and take the 10.17, you'll save yourself £4.50.*
A *Oh, right . . . Thanks.*
B *That's £11.95, please.*
A *Which platform does it go from?*
B *Platform 5.*
A *Do I have to change?*
B *No, it's a through train.*
A *Right, thanks very much.*

a Work in pairs. Read the dialogue.

b Improvise similar dialogues, with different destinations, times and places.

5 🖭 Travel quiz

Form teams of three or four. Listen to the statements on the cassette and discuss whether they are true or false. Score one point for each correct answer.

6 🖭 What's missing?

Listen to the cassette and fill in the missing information in this table.

	Form of transport	Time of departure	Time of arrival	Price
1				
2				
3				

7 Passenger information

Work in pairs. Student A looks at the instructions on this page and student B turns to page 80.

Penzance - Plymouth - Torbay - Exeter - Taunton - London												
	IC	IC	IC	IC	IC		IC		IC	IC	IC	IC R
Mondays to Fridays	✕	✕	✕	✕	✕	∅	**Saturday**		∅	∅	∅	∅
Penzance	—	0646	0953	1150	1625	1730	2245	Penzance			0646	0855
Truro	—	0721	1030	1228	1702	1808	2322	Truro			0721	0929
St Austell	—	0739	1048	1246	1720	1826	2343	St Austell			0739	0947
Bodmin Parkway	—	0754	1103	1304	1738	1844	0001	Bodmin Parkway			0754	1005
Plymouth	0608	0837	1145	1420	1820	1923	0055	Plymouth	0608	0745	0837	1047
Totnes	0635				1847	1953		Totnes	0635	0812		1114
Paignton	—	0850		1425	1820	1924		Paignton		0745		1050
Torquay	—	0855		1431	1825	1929		Torquay		0750		1056
Newton Abbot	0646	0913		1456	1859	2006	0145	Newton Abbot	0646	0824	0913	1126
Exeter St Davids	0707	0938	1240	1517	1920	2035	0220	Exeter St Davids	0707	0845	0938	1147
Tiverton Parkway	0721			1532	1935			Tiverton Parkway	0721	0900		1202
Taunton	0735	1002		1545	1948	2110	0255	Taunton	0735	0913	1002	1215
Westbury	0812				2026			Westbury	0812	0951		1250
Reading (arrive) ➔	0904	1135		1718	2111	2310	0541	Reading (arrive) ➔	0904	1044	1132	1335
London Paddington ↓	0933	1204	1439	1748	2141	2339	0627	London Paddington ↓	0933	1112	1204	1404

KEY ✕ Restaurant-Buffet-Bar ∅ Buffet-Bar IC InterCity train R Seat reservations essential
➔ Railair direct links with Heathrow and Gatwick airports
Light printed timings indicate connecting service

You want to find out the following information from Passenger Travel Enquiries (student B).

1 You live in Bath Spa. You want to be in London by approximately 10.30 tomorrow morning. What time do you have to leave Bath? What time does that train get into London?

2 You live in Weston-super-Mare. You want to be in Reading by not later than 4 p.m. Which train do you have to catch? What time does it arrive? Does that train have a restaurant car?

3 You live near Bristol Parkway station. You want to get to London as early as possible in the morning.

What time does the first train leave? What time does it get to London? Is there an earlier train which leaves from Bristol Temple Meads?

Student B is going to ask you for information which you can answer by looking at the train timetable above. Take it in turns to ask and answer.

Summary of English in situations
• booking into overnight accommodation
• travelling in the UK

1 🎧 Sound right

a Look at these words and mark the most heavily stressed syllable.

Example: p<u>ho</u>tograph

information	pronunciation
interesting	photographer
comfortable	engineer
government	advertisement
telephone	favourite
identity	vegetable
immediately	responsibility

b Now listen and check if you were right. The sound [ə] occurs at least once in each word. Where is it?

2 Language games

Hide your sentence

a Form two teams.

b One member of each team comes to the front of the class. The teacher gives each of them a piece of paper with a sentence written on it.

Examples:
It was the biggest elephant I'd ever seen!
We had egg mayonnaise sandwiches.

c The teacher writes a subject on the board which is related to the sentence, for example, 'zoos'. The two students start a conversation on that subject. They must try to get their sentences into the conversation as naturally as possible. The two teams listen to the conversation and, when the conversation finishes, try to guess what the 'hidden' sentences were. One point for each correct answer.

d The game continues with two new students, different sentences and a new conversation.

3 Read and think

Expert advice

Read this short story and fill each space with one word.

One day a man was (1) . . . his car along a country lane when the engine (2) . . . stopped. He got out of the car, (3) . . . the bonnet and tried to see what was wrong. As he was looking he heard a (4) . . . behind him.

'It's your sparking–plugs. Why don't you clean them?' The man turned (5) . . . and was amazed to see two horses, (6) . . . over the fence. One was black and the (7) . . . white.

'Didn't you (8) . . . me?' said the white horse, 'Your sparking–plugs are dirty.'

Although the man had never (9) . . . a horse talking before he followed the white horse's (10) . . . He took (11) . . . the sparking–plugs and cleaned (12) . . . True enough, after cleaning the plugs the car (13) . . . first time. But when the man looked over the fence both horses had (14) . . . The man got back (15) . . . his car and drove on down the road until he (16) . . . to a pub. He went in and told the barmaid what had (17) . . . 'Was it the black or white horse which (18) . . . to you?' asked the barmaid.

'It was the white one,' (19) . . . the man.

'Oh, that's all right then,' said barmaid. 'The black one doesn't (20) . . . anything about cars.'

4 🎧 Listen to this

Listen to the short conversations on the cassette and write down what the people are talking about. Listen to the example first.

Example: *coffee*

1 ....

2 ....

3 ....

4 ....

5 ....

5 Time to talk

Work in pairs. Student A reads the instructions on this page and student B reads the instructions on page 80.

Look at the pictures on the right. You have half of a story. Student B has the other half. Your pictures are not in the correct order. Describe your pictures to student B. Student B will describe his/her pictures to you. Try to put all ten pictures in the correct order. Then tell the story between you. You must not look at student B's pictures.

6 Work on words

Synonyms

Work in pairs. Student A looks at the words below. Student B looks at the words on page 81.

Try to find words which can mean the same or almost the same as the words on your list. Write down the pairs of synonyms.

Take it in turns to ask and answer. Student A begins.

Example:
Student A *Have you got a word which can mean the same as 'reply'?*
Student B *Yes, I think it's 'answer'.*

reply	hit	annoy
scare	build	choose
mend	demand	carry
raise	convince	grasp
assist	begin	fix
admit	spoil	buy
pursue	hurt	

7 Now you're here

a The following are 'typical' British foods and dishes. Find out what they are. Ask a British person if necessary.

custard	a Cornish pasty
a trifle	Welsh rarebit
a hot pot	Yorkshire pudding
kippers	Worcester sauce
scones	shepherd's pie
a Swiss roll	a ploughman's
HP sauce	baked beans
gravy	

b Observe a British family at mealtimes.

1 What time do they usually have the main meals of the day?
2 Do they normally have anything to drink with their meals?
3 Do they have bread with their meals?
4 How many courses do they have?
5 Do they say anything before they start to eat?
6 Do they usually have meals together?
7 How long does the evening meal usually last?
8 Do they use napkins?
9 Do they have fruit at a meal?
10 Do they have cheese and biscuits?
11 Do they usually have coffee after the meal?
12 How do they leave their knives and forks when they've finished eating?
13 Do they say anything when they leave the table?

What things do you find different or strange about British mealtime customs?

C Compare your answers in class next day.

GRAMMAR IN ACTION

What's typically British?

Breakfast

British people used to sit down to a traditional cooked breakfast which consisted of cereals or porridge, followed by fried eggs, fried bread, sausages, bacon, fried tomatoes, fried mushrooms and even kippers. Then you had toast and marmalade and lots of tea. Nowadays, however, most people just grab a cup of coffee and a piece of toast standing up in the kitchen, before rushing off to school or work. In fact, only one in eight families sit down together for breakfast.

Cricket

This is a complicated outdoor game the English invented, whose rules are virtually impossible for foreign visitors to understand. It is the national summer sport in England. The latest scores in the important matches are given with the news headlines on national radio and television. A match can last up to five days, and even then it often ends in a draw.

Gardening

The British have always loved gardens. Walk down any street on a summer evening and everybody's out watering or weeding. In fact, until television arrived, gardening used to be the most popular hobby in Britain. Many people would say that it still is, but apparently, two out of three Britons consider gardening to be 'outside housework'.

Driving on the left

Until the early nineteenth century, traffic used to drive on the left in most European countries. But nowadays they have all changed over to the right, all except Britain. Fortunately, visitors to Britain soon get used to driving on the 'wrong' side. Unfortunately it takes longer to get used to looking right instead of left when you cross the road.

Fish and chips

Fish and chip shops used to be the only take-away food shops in Britain. The food was wrapped in newspaper and eaten with your fingers. Today there's a lot more choice. People have got used to eating Indian, Chinese, Italian and American 'fast' food.

Summer

The season which sometimes comes to Britain but usually doesn't. But at least the rain gets warmer. August is, in fact, the third wettest month of the year. British people are used to it but they still complain. Older people, in particular, love to grumble about it: 'Summers didn't use to be as bad as this when I was a child!'

Tea

Tea used to be much more popular than coffee. Although much more coffee is drunk now, six out of ten hot drinks consumed in Britain are tea, usually made with tea bags and milk. Many foreigners still believe that the whole country comes to a standstill at 5 o'clock when the British have their tea. Perhaps this used to be true, but not any longer.

1 Right or wrong?

Mark these sentences right (√) or wrong (×).

1 Seven out of eight British families don't have breakfast together.
2 Cricket matches never last longer than five days.
3 One third of Britons actually enjoy gardening.
4 Britain isn't the only European country to drive on the left.
5 There have always been lots of different take-away foods.
6 There are nine months of the year which are drier than August.
7 Coffee is more popular than tea nowadays.

2 Grammar practice

Put *usually, used to, be / get used to* into the gaps in these sentences.

1 I . . . find driving on the left difficult but now I . . . to it.
2 I . . . just have coffee for breakfast so I (not) . . . eating at all before lunch.
3 I . . . take an umbrella with me because it . . . rains if I forget.
4 I still can't . . . fried eggs and bacon in the morning. At home I . . . just have toast.
5 In the 1960's all girls . . . wear miniskirts. Some people were shocked at first, but they soon . . . them.

3 Complete the sentences

Put *the* in these sentences where necessary.

1 Do you like . . . tea with . . . milk in it?
2 . . . old people next door always talk about . . . weather when I see them.
3 . . . majority of . . . English people love . . . gardening.
4 . . . visitors to . . . Britain find it difficult to understand . . . cricket.
5 Who still thinks that . . . men are better drivers than . . . women?

4 Times have changed

Look at these pictures of the 1960's and write sentences like these:

*The Beatles used to be very popular.
A lot of men used to have long hair.*

5 Things in common

a Write down in any order:

● something you used to do but don't do now.
● something you didn't use to do but do now.
● a sport you used to play but don't now.
● a bad habit you used to have but don't have now.
● a food or drink you didn't use to like but do now.
● something naughty you used to do when you were a child.
● something you used to think or believe but don't now.
● a pop group or singer you used to like but don't like now.

b Work in pairs. Show your lists to each other and discuss them. Try to find at least three things which you have in common.

c Tell the rest of the class about the things you have in common.

Example:
*We both used to like Madonna.
We both used to wear Levi 501's.*

6 🔊 The good old days?

Listen to the descriptions on the cassette of how things used to be two hundred years ago. Identify in each case what inventions or discoveries have replaced the things described. There is an example first.

1 . . . .   4 . . . .
2 . . . .   5 . . . .
3 . . . .   6 . . . .

7 Call my bluff

a Work in teams of three. The teacher gives each team an unusual word. They find out and write down what it means. They then write down two false definitions which must include *who, which, that* or *whose*.

b Students in each team read one definition each and the class guess which one is true.

Example:
Student A *A plumber is a person who works on a fruit farm.*
Student B *A plumber is a person who speaks with an upper-class accent.*
Student C *A plumber is a person who installs and repairs water pipes.*

Grammar summary: page 85

1 📺 If you're ill in Britain

At the chemist's

A *Can I help you?*

B *Yes, I've cut my hand and it's very sore. And I've got a pain under my arm.*

A *Yes, that's nasty, isn't it? You need some antibiotics.*

B *Well, can I have some, please?*

A *No, I'm sorry. I can't sell you antibiotics direct. You must go to your doctor first and get a prescription.*

B *But I haven't got a doctor.*

A *In that case you'll have to enrol as a temporary patient with any local GP.*

B *And then do I have to pay for the antibiotics?*

A *Yes, you have to pay the prescription charge, but that isn't as much as the real cost.*

B *I see. Well, thank you very much.*

Making an appointment

B *I'd like to see a doctor, please.*

C *Who is your doctor?*

B *I haven't got one. I'm a foreign student, you see and I'm only in England for three weeks.*

C *Well, in that case, could you fill in this form, please?*

  (pause)

  You're Italian, I see. That means you won't have to pay anything because Italy's in the EEC.
  Now there are four doctors in this practice. Would you like to register with a particular one?

B *No, I don't mind.*

C *Right, I'll put you on Dr Patel's list. I can give you an appointment to see him at 5.15 this evening. Is that all right?*

B *Yes, that's fine, thanks.*

Practise these dialogues in pairs. Change roles.

2 📺 At the doctor's

A *Come in, come in. Miss Rinaldi, isn't it?*

B *Yes, that's right.*

A *Now, what's the problem?*

B *I fell over while I was playing tennis last week and I cut my hand quite badly and it just won't heal.*

A *I see. Well, let me have a look at it . . . Is that painful?*

B *Yes, it is.*

A *And does that hurt?*

B *Yes, it does.*

A *Um, I think you should take a short course of antibiotics to be on the safe side. I'll give you a prescription. It's for some capsules called Floxapen.*

  (pause)

  There we are. Now take this to the nearest chemist's and then take one capsule four times a day, about half an hour before meals.

B *How long for?*

A *For five days.*

B *Right, thank you very much, doctor.*

A *I hope you'll soon feel better. Goodbye.*

Practise the dialogue in pairs. Then improvise a similar conversation without looking in the book. Invent your own symptoms.

3 What's wrong with you?

a In groups, one student at a time chooses and then mimes one of the symptoms or complaints below. The rest of the group guess what's wrong.

You can feel	dizzy.
	faint.
	stiff.
	sick.
	feverish.
	shivery.

You can have a pain in your	stomach.
	shoulder.
	chest.
	throat, etc.

Your	shoulder neck, etc.	can	ache.
			be sore.
			be painful.

You can have	an infection.
	the flu.
	a temperature.
	a cough.
	backache.
	earache.
	a headache.
	a rash.
	a runny nose.
	hay fever.
	a (bad) cold.
	an upset stomach.
	a hangover.

b 🖃
A *You don't look very well. Are you feeling OK?*
B *No, I'm feeling awful. I've got a temperature and I ache all over.*
A *Oh, I'm sorry. Why don't you take a couple of aspirins?*
B *I tried that but they didn't do any good at all.*
A *Well, in that case you ought to see a doctor.*

Work in pairs. One person describes how he/she's feeling using the symptoms and phrases above, the other gives advice using these phrases:

You should/ought to . . .
Why don't you . . . ?
Why not . . . ?
If I were you, I'd . . .

4 🖃 What's wrong?

Listen to two conversations in the doctor's surgery. Then fill in the missing information below.

Problems?

How long for?

What's wrong?

Prescription?

Treatment / Advice

Summary of English in situations

- describing what's wrong with you
- making a doctor's appointment
- at the doctor's

1 🎧 Sound right

a Read these sentences.

Where do you want to go for lunch?

He was swimming in the sea when he saw a huge shark.

Underline the words which you think are stressed.

b Now listen to the sentences on the cassette. Which words were stressed? Are they the same as the words you underlined? What sort of words are normally stressed? Which are normally unstressed?

c Underline the stressed words in these sentences.

Can you lend me your pen?

We can go to Bath next week if you like.

My feet are warm but my hands are cold.

Check your answers by listening to the cassette.

d Now listen to these pairs of sentences. Which words in them are stressed?

I can speak French.
I can't speak French.

We're late.
We aren't late.

I've had my lunch.
I haven't had my lunch.

You must speak to them.
You mustn't speak to them.

Practise saying the sentences. Make sure you stress the negative words.

e Listen to some pairs of sentences on the cassette and mark them with a tick if they are positive, a cross if they are negative.

1 .... 2 .... 3 .... 4 ....
5 .... 6 .... 7 .... 8 ....

2 Work on words

Match the idioms with their explanations.

Example: 1 – h

1 It rings a bell.
2 I'll give you a lift.
3 I'll give you a ring.
4 Make up your mind!
5 It's up to you.
6 You're pulling my leg!
7 I really put my foot in it.
8 I haven't got a clue.
9 I'm completely broke.
10 Are you on the phone?
11 Let's go halves.
12 It serves you right!
13 You're kidding!
14 What a rip off!
15 I don't fancy it.

a) You decide/choose.
b) You're joking!
c) I haven't got any money at all.
d) You deserve(d) to suffer.
e) I made an embarrassing mistake.
f) We can pay for it between us.
g) I don't want to do it.
h) It sounds familiar to me.
i) It's not worth the money./They're cheating us.
j) I have no idea.
k) You're making fun of me.
l) Have you got a phone?
m) I'll phone you.
n) I'll take you in my car.
o) Decide!

3 Language games

Twenty questions

a Student 1 writes down a word on a piece of paper. It can be:

an object, for example, *a camera*
a person, for example, *a nurse*
a place, for example, *a library*.

b The teacher checks the word and student 1 tells the class 'object', 'person' or 'place'.

c The class can ask a maximum of 20 questions to guess the word. Student 1 can only answer 'yes' or 'no', or 'sometimes'.

Example:
Student 1 *'Person'*.
Student 2 *Does this person work indoors?*
Student 3 *Does this person work in an office?*
Student 4 *Does this person work with computers?*

d The student who correctly guesses the word chooses the next one. If no one guesses the word, student 1 wins and chooses a new student 1.

4 🎧 Listen to this

You are going to hear a story about a man who returns to his home town after many years and finds that everything there has changed. As you listen, think about the answers to these questions.

1 Why had George Cox been away from his home town?
2 How long had he been away?
3 What had happened to George's old house?
4 Where did he go for a cup of tea?
5 What mistake did he make there?
6 Why did he go back to the old shoemaker's?
7 What happened there?

5 Read and think

The cynic's dictionary

a These words and definitions from a 'dictionary' have become mixed up. Match the definitions on the right with the correct words on the left.

Example: 1 – f

1	star	a)	Something you just tell one person at a time.
2	bank	b)	Whoosh — and then walk a mile.
3	business	c)	A large piece of paper which tells you everything you want to know except how to fold it up again.
4	friend	d)	A book with a photo you laugh at without realizing that this is the way your friends see you.
5	tourist	e)	A place where you can borrow money if you can convince them you don't really need it.
6	mother	f)	A person who works hard all his life to become famous, then wears dark glasses to avoid being recognized.
7	passport	g)	Someone who dislikes the same people as you.
8	road map	h)	Someone who can look in a drawer and find socks that aren't there.
9	secret	i)	How to get other people's money without violence.
10	skiing	j)	Someone who travels to see things which are different and then complains when they're not the same.

b Now work in groups. Think of similar definitions for five of the words in the box.

a bath	hair	love	a computer
Sunday	toast	an umbrella	
money	a cigarette	a policeman	

6 Time to talk

a Choose three of the following occasions and make notes about what happened.

- A time when you felt really scared.
- A time when something happened which made you laugh a lot.
- An amazing coincidence which happened to you.
- A situation which made you really lose your temper.
- A time when you were very surprised or shocked.
- A situation when you felt extremely embarrassed.

b In groups describe your experiences in as much detail as possible. Ask each other questions to build up a complete picture of each situation.

7 Now you're here

Ask a British person the following questions.

1 How many hours do you work a week?
2 How many hours do you watch TV in the evening?
3 Do you do much DIY?
4 How often do you go out in the evenings?
5 How often do you go to:
   a) the cinema
   b) the theatre
   c) a concert
   d) bingo?
6 How often do you eat in a restaurant?
7 How often do you go to a pub?
8 Do you ever have or go to parties?
9 Are you a member of any clubs or societies?
10 Do you ever go dancing? (What sort of dancing?)
11 Do you take part in any sport? (Which sports? How often?)
12 Do you watch any sports live or on TV?

UNIT NINE
· LESSON ONE

Don't just listen — watch!

When we meet someone for the first time, it's no use trying to hide how we feel about them. Psychologists say that we can't help showing our true attitudes towards the other person, even if we actually say very little.

So how can you tell whether people like you or not? Or, perhaps more importantly, if you want to know if a particular person finds you attractive or not, what are the signs to look for?

Psychologists say it's easy to tell. All you need to do is to keep watching him or her very carefully, to find out how they feel about you. Their 'body language' will give them away.

These are the signs you should look for:

You can tell that the other person likes you if he:

- looks you in the eye, without blinking or looking away.
- seems to have large pupils in his eyes.
- tries to improve his appearance by touching his hair or clothes all the time.
- stands or sits straight in front of you, or leans forward to talk or listen to you.
- stands close to you, pulls in his stomach and pushes out his chest.

You can tell that the other person doesn't find you attractive if she:

- avoids looking you in the eye, or looks away when you try to make eye contact.
- seems to have very small pupils in her eyes.
- folds her arms or crosses her legs.
- stands sideways to you or keeps her distance.
- leans backwards away from you.
- points her knees away from you when she's sitting.

So you'd better be careful if you don't want people to know how you feel about them. But if you want somebody to know that you like them and that you enjoy being with them, you don't have to say anything – you should just let your body talk!

1 Who likes who?

Read the text and then look at each picture carefully and write down how you know that:

A he is attracted to her but she isn't attracted to him
B she is attracted to him but he isn't attracted to her
C they are both attracted to each other
D neither of them is attracted to the other.

Example:
B *She's leaning forwards to talk to him but he's looking away.*

2 Do as I say

Imagine you're sitting opposite someone of the opposite sex. Listen to the voice on the cassette. You will hear a series of instructions. Do exactly what those instructions tell you to do.

3 Grammar practice

Use the verbs in brackets in the infinitive (*to meet*) or the gerund (*meeting*).

Examples:
I'm pleased to meet you.
I'm looking forward to meeting you.
You look tired. You should go to bed.

1 I'm not very good at (dance) so I'm afraid of (ask) him (go) to a disco.
2 Do you want (meet) him?
   Yes, I'm very interested in (hear) about his trip to Peru.
3 I like (dance) but I'm tired of (dance) with him.
4 They went on (stare) into each other's eyes without (say) anything.
5 I'm fed up with (wait) for her (finish)(talk).
6 My parents (make) me go on holiday with them.
7 Don't (let) him (tell) you what (do).

4 About your partner

a Work in pairs. How well do you know your partner? On your own write sentences about him/her using the phrases in the box.

He's/She's	interested tired good fond fed up bad frightened afraid keen	about in on of at with

b Now talk to each other about the things you wrote about in a). Ask and answer questions like this:

A *What are you interested in?*
B *I'm interested in travelling and meeting new people.*
B *What are you good at?*
A *I'm good at listening to other people's problems.*

5 More body language

a In your country how do you demonstrate the following phrases using body language, signs and gestures?

I'm tired.   Be quiet.   I'm bored.
I've got a headache.   I'm freezing.
He's stupid.   I don't know.
Do you want a drink?   I'm scared.
Hurry up.   I'm fed up with waiting.
There's someone on the phone for you.

b Now work in groups. Think of other things which you can 'say' by using body language. Demonstrate them to the rest of the class as in a).

Grammar summary: page 85

1 What do they mean?

a Work in pairs. Take it in turns to explain what these signs mean.

Use these phrases:

You must . . .
You have to . . .
You mustn't . . .
You can't . . .
You don't have to . . .
You're not allowed to . . .

No bill - sticking

Queue here

Mon - Sat
8am - 6.30pm

Please do not ask for credit as a refusal may offend.

Trespassers will be prosecuted.

Service included

Do not talk to the driver or distract his attention while vehicle is in motion.

40

The management retains the right to refuse entry.

Communication cord.
Penalty for improper use £50.

No fouling of footpaths.
Penalty £20.

HOTEL BAR
Open to non-residents

STOP

2 Which sign?

Listen to the cassette and decide which of the signs they are talking about.

KEEP CLEAR

STOP CHILDREN

1 ....

2 ....

3 ....

4 ....

5 ....

GIVE WAY

Shoplifters will be prosecuted.

6 ....

7 ....

b Where do you usually see these signs?

c Can you remember any other signs you've seen? Were they difficult to understand? Write them down. Compare them with other pairs.

3 How much do you know?

Form two teams. Discuss the following and tick each one according to whether you think it is true or false in Britain.

- ☐ School teachers are not allowed to hit pupils.
- ☐ Everybody with a job has to make a tax declaration every year.
- ☐ You have to vote in general elections.
- ☐ You don't have to wear a helmet when you ride a motorbike or moped.
- ☐ You have to have a passport to travel in another country in the EEC.
- ☐ If you've got a television, you have to have a TV licence.
- ☐ You are not allowed to cycle on the pavement.
- ☐ Military service is compulsory.
- ☐ Parents are not allowed to hit their children.
- ☐ If you go to university, you get a grant which you have to repay.
- ☐ You have to have a licence to ride a moped.
- ☐ If you own a dog, you must have a dog licence.

- ☐ If your car is more than three years old, you must have it tested to make sure it is safe.
- ☐ If you've got a hosepipe in your garden, you must have a special licence.
- ☐ It is compulsory to carry an identity card.
- ☐ School is compulsory between the ages of five and sixteen.
- ☐ Passengers in the front and back seats of cars have to wear seat belts.

4 Make comparisons

a Make a list of six laws or customs which are different in Britain and in your country.

Example:
In Britain you mustn't drive at more than 70 mph on motorways.
In Germany we're allowed to drive as fast as we like.

b Discuss your answers in groups, preferably with students of different nationalities.

5 Unwritten 'rules'

a Form groups of three or four students. In your groups discuss the unwritten 'rules' for three of the situations below. Use these verbs and phrases:

should	*shouldn't*
must	*mustn't*
have to	*don't have to*
are allowed to	*aren't allowed to*
can	*can't*

- meeting a British person for the first time
- eating with a British family
- in your summer school class
- at a party or disco in Britain
- being a pedestrian in Britain
- shopping in Britain

Example:
You don't have to shake hands when you meet new people.

b Think of another situation in Britain where there are unwritten 'rules'. Make a list of them. Then discuss your list with other groups.

Summary of English in situations

- talking about rules, regulations and obligations

1 🎧 Sound right

a Listen to this phrase. It is repeated five times. Each time a different word is heavily stressed. Number the word you hear stressed. The first one has been done for you.

I
I wanted to buy a new car

b The meaning of the phrase changes when a different word is stressed. Listen again and make a complete sentence with one of the phrases below.

- ☐ a) not a motorbike.
- ☐ b) but my wife didn't.
- ☐ c) not an old one.
- ☐ d) but I didn't have enough money.
- ☐ e) not hire one.

c Now practise saying the whole sentences.

d Listen to the following six sentences and try to finish them in a natural way. Write down your answers.

Example:
I thought he was French, but he was Italian.

2 Read and think

Work in small groups. Try to work out the answers to these problems.

1 Two airline pilots were flying a jumbo jet to New York. The one on the left was the father of the other one's son. How was this possible?

2 Two men were standing in a field. One was looking north and the other was looking south. How could they see each other without turning round?

3 In your country, would it be legal for you to marry your widow's sister?

4 A dark-skinned man wearing dark trousers and a dark sweater was walking down the middle of a narrow country road. Suddenly a black car with no lights on came round the corner at high speed. How did the car manage to avoid hitting the man?

5 My father's got one child. Who is my father's child's daughter's brother?

6 If you pronounce 'gh' as in 'cough', 'o' as in 'women' and 'ti' as in 'station', how would you pronounce 'ghoti'?

3 Work on words

Complete the sentences using the words in the box, making them into *-ed* or *-ing* adjectives.

> embarrass surprise excite shock
> worry disappoint bore
> horrify disgust tire depress
> interest

Example:
Last night's football match was very . . .
Last night's football match was very exciting.

1 Are you . . . in astrology? There's a documentary on television tonight.
2 The exam results were very . . . We were all . . .
3 Her boyfriend is so . . . All he talks about is computers.
4 Everybody was . . . when they heard about the . . . accident.
5 You look . . . Why don't you go to bed?
6 I felt so . . . when I fell off my chair in the restaurant – everybody laughed.
7 Stop picking your nose – it's a . . . habit.
8 The news was . . . and we are all very . . . about it.

4 🎧 Listen to this

The streets of London

Read the lyrics to this song and try to predict what the missing words are. Then listen to the cassette and write down the correct word for each space.

Have you seen the old man in the closed down . . .
Kicking up the papers with his worn out . . .
In his eyes you see no . . .
and held loosely by his side,
Yesterday's paper,
telling yesterday's . . .

So how can you tell me you're . . .
And say for you that the sun don't . . .
Let me take you by the . . .
and lead you through the streets of London. I'll show you something to make you change your . . .

Have you seen the old girl who . . . the streets of London?
Dirt in her hair and her . . . in rags.
She's no time for . . . she just keeps right on walking, carrying her . . . in two carrier bags.

Chorus

In the all-night cafe at a . . . past eleven,
Same old man sitting there on his . . .
Looking at the . . . over the rim of his tea cup. Each tea . . . an hour and he wanders home . . .

Chorus

5 Language games

Think fast

a Form teams of three or four students.

b The teacher reads out a sentence starting 'Think of six things . . .'

c The teams think of six possible answers and write them down. When the list is complete they shout out BINGO! The first team to finish score a point.

Example:
Teacher *Think of six things you can do with a brick.*

Team A's list *Use it for a doorstop, a paper weight, a smash and grab jewellery raid, a mouse's headstone, to stop a car rolling downhill and as a sunbed for a kitten.*

6 Time to talk

clocks   the microscope   television
the computer   printing   the wheel
gunpowder   the motor car
the telephone   paper

a Work in pairs and put the above inventions in chronological order, starting with the earliest invention.

b In your pairs choose three inventions from the list that you think have had the most positive effect on civilization and three inventions that you think have had the most negative effect.

c Now join another pair. Look at your lists together and discuss them until you agree on the three most positive and most negative inventions.

d Read out your lists to the class and try to produce final class lists of positive and negative inventions.

7 Now you're here

Do you know these signs and notices? Fill in the missing word for each one. Ask a British person to help you or go out into the street and look for them.

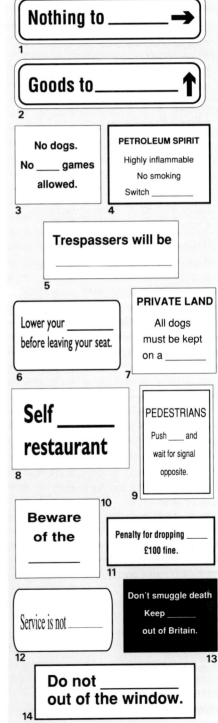

Nothing to _____ ➔
1

Goods to_____ ↑
2

No dogs.
No ____ games allowed.
3

PETROLEUM SPIRIT
Highly inflammable
No smoking
Switch _____
4

Trespassers will be
_____
5

Lower your _____
before leaving your seat.
6

PRIVATE LAND
All dogs must be kept on a _____
7

Self _____ restaurant
8

PEDESTRIANS
Push ____ and wait for signal opposite.
9

Beware of the
_____
10, 11

Penalty for dropping _____
£100 fine.
11

Service is not _____
12

Don't smuggle death
Keep _____
out of Britain.
13

Do not _____ out of the window.
14

59

UNIT TEN · LESSON ONE

GRAMMAR IN ACTION

A day at the seaside

Brighton is situated on the south coast of England, 97 kms from London. It was made fashionable by the Royal family in the late eighteenth century. The most famous building in Brighton, the Royal Pavilion, was built in 1787.

Although it is unique in many ways, Brighton is also a typical English seaside resort. In an average year, it is visited by over 1.3 million holiday-makers, and its 30 language schools are attended by more than 25,000 foreign students.

So, what happens there on a typical day in August?

10 a.m.
Thousands of traditional English breakfasts have been eaten by the guests at the many bed-and-breakfasts and small hotels all over the town.

11 a.m.
The town has already been invaded by huge crowds of day trippers. Hundreds of deck-chairs are being hired on the beach and seafront. Kiss-me-quick hats and tubes of sun cream are being bought by optimistic sunbathers.

1 p.m.
Hundreds of portions of fish and chips and hamburgers are being served by the beach cafes and fast-food places near the seafront.

5 p.m.
Thousands of red-nosed sun-bathers have been forced to leave the beach by the incoming tide.

Fortunes have been spent in the amusement arcades on and near the pier, and a lot of fortunes have been told by 'genuine' gypsy fortune tellers – but how many of them will come true?

10 p.m.
Dozens of foreign languages are being spoken in the discos by students who are in Brighton to learn English.

Live music can be heard pouring out from pubs and clubs in the narrow streets behind the seafront.

By midnight, most of the day trippers have gone. Soon the inhabitants of Brighton will be left in relative peace . . . until tomorrow.

1 Make true sentences

Make eleven true sentences.

Example:
Brighton is visited by over 1.3 million holiday-makers.

Brighton		(spend)	to leave the beach.
Thousands of English		(force)	in the clubs and discos.
Breakfasts	is	(visit)	by 'gypsy' fortune tellers.
The Royal Pavilion		(invade)	in the amusement arcades.
Dozens of foreign	are	(make)	by over 1.3 million holiday-makers.
languages		(tell)	by crowds of day trippers.
Fortunes	was	(build)	on the beach and seafront.
Sunbathers		(hire)	by foreign students.
Deck-chairs	were	(play)	by bed-and-breakfast guests.
Live music		(eat)	famous by the Royal family.
Fortunes		(speak)	in 1787.

2 What is it?

One student at a time thinks of an object. The rest of the class ask questions (which must be in the passive) to find out what the object is.

Examples of questions:

What's it made of?
Where's it usually found?
Can it be bought in a shop?
Can it be eaten?
Can it be broken?
Can it be bent?
Can it be carried?
Is it ever worn?
Could it be hidden, under a bed, for example?
Is it ever sent by post?

3 What's missing?

Work in pairs. Student A reads the instructions below, student B reads the instructions on page 81.

a There are ten gaps in this description of the Royal Pavilion in Brighton. Write ten questions to ask student B to find out the missing information.

Example:
When was the original farmhouse bought?

b Ask student B your questions and answer his/her questions.

The Royal Pavilion was originally a small farmhouse. In (1) . . . it was bought by George III's son, the Prince of Wales. Then, bit by bit, it was expanded into one of the most extraordinary buildings in Britain.

In 1787 extra rooms were added so the house was big enough for the Prince's (2) . . . In the early years of the 1800's more rooms and (3) . . . were added in all directions and the main rooms were redecorated in a Chinese style. Then, in 1805, plans were made to change the whole exterior to a (4) . . . style. At the last minute these plans were changed and an Indian style was decided on instead because at that time India and all things Indian were fashionable (India was then the jewel in the British Empire.)

Between 1808 and (5) . . . a riding school and stables were built and two huge new rooms were added, all in the new Indian style. This final change of style was designed by (6) . . . , the architect of Buckingham Palace. A lot of new technology was used in the construction of the Pavilion and it was the first building in the world to be lit by (7) . . . It was also centrally heated which, at that time, was revolutionary.

When the Prince of Wales became (8) . . . in 1820, he was 58 and very overweight and the Royal Pavilion was used less and less. He died ten years later.

In the 1840's most of the contents of the Pavilion were (9) . . . and the building was nearly demolished. It wasn't until the 1920's that it began to be restored and its contents (10) . . .

4 General knowledge quiz

Form two teams. Listen to the general knowledge questions on the cassette. Team A answer question 1, team B question 2, etc. Teams have 30 seconds to discuss each question and decide on the answer.

Grammar summary: page 86

I 📼 First meeting

A *Do you want to dance?*
B *Yes, OK.*

(later)

Shall we sit down?
A *Yes, good idea.*
B *Can I get you a drink?*
A *Yes, please.*
B *What would you like?*
A *A shandy, please.*

(later)

A *Can I give you a lift home?*
B *No, it's OK, thanks. I can take a taxi.*
A *Are you sure?*
B *Oh, all right then.*

(later)

A *Are you on the phone?*
B *Yes, I am. My number's 788032.*
A *I'll ring you sometime then.*
B *Yes, OK. Goodnight. Thanks for the lift.*
A *Goodnight.*

a Practise the dialogue in pairs.

b Change the underlined phrases to:

Would you like to dance?
Shall we have a dance?

Yes, | *all right.*
      | *let's.*

Let's sit down.

Yes, | *OK.*
      | *all right.*

Would you like a drink?
Do you want something to drink?
What do you want?
What will you have?

2 📼 Excuses, excuses . . .

Listen to the conversation on the cassette and then fill in the table below.

	Mark's suggestion	Sarah's excuse
Tuesday		
Wednesday		
Thursday		
Friday		
Saturday		

3 Keep trying

Work in pairs. Student A reads the instructions below. Student B reads the instructions on page 81.

You fancy student B. Phone and invite him/her to:

1 play tennis with you this afternoon.
2 go to a pizza restaurant this evening.
3 go sailing tomorrow afternoon.
4 go to a party tomorrow evening.
5 go to the beach the day after.
6 go to a rock concert next Saturday.

Keep trying. He/She will probably say yes to one of your suggestions. Use phrases like:

Do you want to . . . ?
Would you like to . . . ?

How | *about . . . ?*
What |

Do you | *fancy* | *. . . ?*
| *feel like* |

4 Dos and don'ts in pubs

Pubs are a unique British institution. There are some customs concerning pubs which are useful to know about.

Do . . .

- pay for your drink at the same time as you order it, not at the end of the evening.
- order drinks in rounds if you're with a group of friends.
- have money ready in your hand, especially in a crowded pub.
- ask if a seat or table is free before you sit down.
- say 'Thanks.' and 'Goodbye.' or 'Goodnight.' when you leave.

Don't . . .

- get drunk.
- sit down and wait for someone to come and serve you. They won't!
- buy an alcoholic drink unless you're 18.
- drink and drive.
- just ask for 'a beer'. You must specify a type of beer and if you want 'a half' or 'a pint'.
- give the person behind the bar a tip (but you can buy him/her a drink.)
- make too much noise in the lounge bar.
- sit all evening over one drink (you won't be very welcome next time if you do.)

5 What are they doing wrong?

Listen to people 'ignoring' some of the customs above. Write down what they're doing wrong.

1 ....
2 ....
3 ....
4 ....
5 ....
6 ....
7 ....
8 ....

Summary of English in situations
<ul><li>inviting</li><li>accepting and refusing invitations</li><li>going to pubs</li></ul>

1 ⊟ Sound right

a Look at the following questions. Listen to them on the cassette. Do the speakers' voices rise ↗ or fall ↘?

1 Are you tired?
2 Is she French?
3 Have you got the time?
4 Can you play chess?
5 Am I late?
6 Do you like English?

b Listen again and repeat after the cassette.

c Now listen to these six questions. Do the speakers' voices rise ↗ or fall ↘?

1 What's your name?
2 How are you?
3 When's the party?
4 Where are my books?
5 Which one's yours?
6 Why are you crying?

d Listen again and repeat after the cassette.

e Now listen to eight questions on the cassette. Put a ↗ if the speaker's voice rises, and a ↘ if his/her voice falls.

1	....	5	....
2	....	6	....
3	....	7	....
4	....	8	....

f Listen again and check your answers. Practise saying the questions with the correct rising or falling intonation.

2 Read and think

a Read this story carefully.

A man was standing on the platform at Victoria station. He had an enormous suitcase with him. He wanted to go to Brighton but he didn't want to buy a ticket – he was too mean, and didn't like spending money.

When the train arrived he got on and sat down, putting the suitcase on the seat opposite him. The train left London and after about twenty minutes the ticket collector came round.

When he arrived at the man with the big suitcase he said:
   'Can I see your ticket please, sir?'
   'I'm sorry,' replied the man. 'I haven't got one. I seem to have lost it.' But of course the ticket collector didn't believe him.
   'I know your type. You're just too mean to buy a ticket. You'll have to pay £20.' he said to the man. 'That's double the normal price of the fare.'
   'I haven't got £20,' replied the man. 'I haven't got any money at all.' And then he started laughing.

When the man laughed, the ticket collector completely lost his temper.

b What do you think happened next? Working in pairs complete the story. Compare the different endings with the rest of the class.

3 Work on words

a Work in pairs. Which word or phrase in each group does not go with the other three? Explain why it is the odd word out.

Example:
moped (bike) scooter motorbike

'Bike' is the odd word out because it doesn't have an engine.

b Compare your answers with other pairs.

1	niece	9	backpack
	cousin		sleeping bag
	aunt		suitcase
	mother-in-law		carrier bag
2	wall	10	receipt
	hedge		tip
	path		bill
	fence		menu
3	lane	11	dizzy
	street		faint
	motorway		headache
	road		sick
4	zip	12	chat show
	belt		documentary
	collar		soap opera
	button		comedy
5	cup	13	try on
	plate		look after
	glass		put on
	mug		take off
6	starter	14	to stir
	salad		to fry
	main course		to grill
	dessert		to boil
7	driver's licence	15	to cough
	identity card		to sneeze
	passport		to yawn
	credit card		to sniff
8	waste paper bin	16	to clap
	bread bin		to wave
	litter bin		to kick
	dust bin		to scratch

4 Language games

Make noises

a Form two teams, A and B.

b Each team discusses the meaning of the verbs below. They all involve making a noise.

whistle	pant	hum
sigh	cheer	sneeze
yawn	swallow	clear your throat
breathe	sing	sigh
shout	cough	gasp
scream	hiccup	sob
whisper	blow	blow your nose
groan	boo	sniff
snore	mumble	

c Team A choose five verbs and write them down. Five members of the team demonstrate one verb each, one after another, very quickly.

d Team B discuss what they have heard and say which verbs were demonstrated and in which order.

e Team B now choose five verbs and the game continues.

f Score one point for naming each verb and five points for putting them in the correct order.

5 🎧 Listen to this

Listen to this excerpt from a radio programme. Then number these sentences from 1 – 12, in the order in which they happened.

☐ Charlie went through the departure gate.

☐ Laura introduced Charlie to her parents.

☐ Charlie decided to emigrate.

☐ Charlie left school.

☐ Laura and Charlie fell in love.

☐ Laura's father disapproved of Charlie.

☐ Laura found the kitten.

☐ Charlie arranged to leave Laura a present.

☐ Laura started to go out with Charlie.

☐ Laura played the old 60's hit record.

☐ Laura's parents realized she wasn't studying as hard as she should.

☐ Laura and Charlie met in secret.

6 Time to talk

a In pairs or groups match the crimes in the box to the descriptions below.

> vandalism tax evasion blackmail
> hooliganism mugging theft
> drinking and driving shoplifting
> armed robbery kidnapping

1 Attacking someone in the street, and taking his/her watch and £20.
2 Breaking a public telephone and covering the phone box with graffiti.
3 Stealing clothes worth £50 from a department store.
4 Driving a car after drinking four whiskies.
5 Fighting with rival supporters during a football match.
6 Robbing a bank of £20,000 after threatening to use a gun.
7 Stealing a child and demanding money for its safe return.
8 Cheating the taxman out of £50,000.
9 Stealing a radio cassette player from a car.
10 Demanding payment in return for not revealing embarrassing or incriminating facts.

b Write down what you think are the three most serious crimes, and the three least serious crimes. Compare your answers with other groups, and discuss the differences.

7 Now you're here

Find out how law-abiding the average Briton is by asking a British person these questions:

1 If you're a pedestrian, do you cross the road at traffic lights when the pedestrian light is on red?
2 Do you ever travel on a bus or train without paying for the ticket?
3 If you're driving, do you ever go through traffic lights when they're amber or red?
4 When you're in a car, do you always wear a seat belt?
5 When you're driving, by how much do you break the speed limit in towns and on motorways?
6 If you smoke, do you ever smoke in non-smoking areas, for example, in a cinema?
7 Do you ever drop litter in the street?
8 If you own a dog, and it fouls the pavement, do you clean up after it?
9 Do you ever leave your car at home and use public transport if you're going to a party and you know you'll drink some alcohol?
10 Do you declare everything you bring back from abroad? (What sort of things do you not declare?)

Make notes of the answers you get and compare them in class the next day.

UNIT ELEVEN
LESSON ONE

GRAMMAR IN ACTION

What would have happened?

Lucky Break

A young drummer called Richard put an advertisement in the evening newspaper in Liverpool. It said 'Pop drummer available for work with local group.'

That evening the phone rang. It was the manager of a group who offered him a job for £5 a night. Richard said he would think about it and ring back.

Half an hour later, a member of another group phoned up and said he would pay Richard £2 more if he played for them. Richard agreed to join them. He made the right decision.

If he'd accepted the first offer, his whole life would have been very different. Richard Starkey later changed his name to Ringo Starr. The name of the second group was *The Beatles*.

Penalty!

Nick French was walking home from work one afternoon when he heard a child screaming. He looked up and saw three-year-old Sharon Collins hanging, terrified, from a balcony four floors above him. She had climbed over to try to rescue her cat and then couldn't get back. As Nick watched, horrified, Sharon lost her grip and fell. Without thinking Nick ran forwards, dived and caught Sharon in his arms. The child was shocked but unhurt.

A police spokesperson said later, 'Sharon shouldn't have been playing on the balcony. If Nick hadn't been passing at that moment she would have been killed, for certain. It was a magnificent catch!'

Nick commented modestly, 'I'm the goalkeeper in a local football team. I haven't been playing very well lately. That must have been the best save I've made all season!'

1 Make true sentences

Example: 1 – g

1 Sharon wouldn't have climbed over the balcony
2 If Nick hadn't heard Sharon screaming,
3 Sharon would've been killed
4 If Nick hadn't been a goalkeeper,
5 If Richard had said 'yes' to the first offer,
6 Richard wouldn't have been in the 'Beatles'
7 If Richard hadn't been a drummer,

a) if Nick hadn't walked by.
b) he wouldn't have become rich and famous.
c) if he'd taken the first job.
d) he wouldn't have got the job.
e) he wouldn't have looked up.
f) he wouldn't have caught Sharon.
g) if she hadn't wanted to rescue the cat.

2 Grammar practice

Choose verbs to complete these sentences. Think carefully about the tenses. A (−) indicates that you should use a negative.

Example:
If Nick . . . (−) Sharon, he . . . (−) her.
If Nick hadn't seen Sharon, he wouldn't have rescued her.

1 If Nick . . . half a minute later, Sharon . . .
2 Sharon . . . (−) on the balcony if the cat . . . (−)
3 If Sharon . . . (−), Nick . . . (−) her.
4 Ringo . . . the first group if the 'Beatles' . . . (−) him more money.
5 If Ringo . . . the first group, he . . . (−) famous.

3 What's missing?

Complete the sentences with *should, shouldn't, should've* or *shouldn't have* and a verb in the correct tense. A (−) indicates that you should make a negative sentence.

Example:
I'm sorry. I . . . (−) at you like that last night.
I'm sorry. I shouldn't have shouted at you like that last night.

1 You look ill. You . . . to bed.
2 It was a fantastic concert yesterday. You . . .
3 You . . . (−) so much. It's very unhealthy.
4 It's your fault! You . . . (−) the door unlocked last night.
5 We're lost! I'm sure we . . . right about half an hour ago.
6 The tickets are sold out. We . . . them yesterday.
7 I . . . more exercise. I'm overweight.

4 If only . . .

a Listen to a story on the cassette and make notes of what happened.

b In pairs retell the story using your notes.

c Now listen to the first half of seven sentences about the story and choose the correct ending for each one from a – g below.

Example:
1 – a

a) . . . he wouldn't have shouted to his father.
b) . . . they might have sunk.
c) . . . none of all this would have happened.
d) . . . he wouldn't have twisted his ankle.
e) . . . the car would have landed on top of her.
f) . . . he wouldn't have caught his trouser leg in the handbrake.
g) . . . the car wouldn't have landed on top of it.

5 What's the story?

a Read the following newspaper headlines and say what you think happened in each story.

b Make a conditional sentence for each explanation using *If* . . .

Example:

Goalkeeper saves girl in balcony fall

a) *The story is about a girl who fell off a balcony and was caught by a goalkeeper who was passing at that moment.*
b) *If the goalkeeper hadn't caught the girl, she would've been killed.*

Rock singer in skiing accident - misses concert
1

Tennis star loses temper . . . and match
2

FORGETFUL POOLS 'WINNER' LOSES A MILLION
3

Crops fail in summer scorcher
4

6 What must've happened?

Listen to the sounds and voices on the cassette and say what must have happened.

Example:
Somebody must've scored a goal.

7 Telepathy

a Form two or three teams. One member of each team sits at the front of the class with his / her back to the team. Team members take it in turns to be the team 'leader'.

b Each team leader writes an ending to the first of the unfinished sentences below. The + or – indicates if the ending has to be positive or negative.

c Individually the other team members try to guess what their leader has written and write down the same ending to the sentence (without speaking to or copying from their team mates).

d The teams score one point for every member who has written the same as their leader.

Example:
You wouldn't be so tired today if you . . . (+)

. . . *had gone to bed earlier.*

1 If you'd remembered the map, we . . . (+)
2 If you hadn't missed that goal, we . . . (−)
3 I would've sent you a card if I . . . (+)
4 I wouldn't have found out the truth if you . . . (−)
5 If you hadn't arrived at college late everyday, you . . . (−)

Grammar summary: page 86

1 What's on?

Look at these programmes which were on television on one particular evening in Britain.

Television Programme Guide

BBC 1

7.00 Wogan Guests: Dustin Hoffman and Joan Armatrading.

7.30 Wildlife on One David Attenborough among the Falkland Islands' penguins and sea lions.

8.00 Dynasty Alexis drives Dex away.

8.50 Points of View Comments on programmes - for and against.

9.00 News; regional news; weather.

9.30 Panorama No Spring in Prague: communism in Czechoslovakia.

10.10 Miami Vice Crockett and Tubbs investigate a porn film racket.

11.00 Ballroom Dancing Championships

ITV

7.00 Surprise Surprise More big prizes to be won.

7.30 Coronation Street Shirley tries hard to avoid Curly.

8.00 The Bill A prisoner turns police informer.

8.30 After Henry Sarah decides to go to Paris, with hilarious results.

9.00 Heroes Australian World War II drama with Jason Donovan.

10.00 News at Ten; weather.

10.30 Football FA Cup Semi-Finals.

11.35 Donahue Studio discussion on why some yuppies leave the rat race.

BBC 2

7.00 Open to Question Documentary followed by studio discussion. 'Do we need vigilantes on our streets and on the underground?'

7.40 The Education Programme Public schools go co-educational.

8.30 Gardener's World

9.00 Film 'Live and Let Die' with Roger Moore as James Bond.

11.00 Newsnight The British economy

11.45 Snub New, progressive music

C4

7.00 Channel 4 News, weather.

7.50 Comment A personal view of the news.

8.00 Brookside Tracy tries to resign, and Harry argues with Kevin.

8.30 Treasure Hunt This week's location is Cornwall.

9.30 Film on 4 'A Room with a View', with Maggie Smith.

11.30 Ice Skating World Speed Skating Championships.

Write down the names of one or more programmes in each of the categories below.

chat show	game show
documentary	sports programme
sitcom	variety show
soap opera	music programme
play	crime series
current affairs programme	natural history programme

2 What to watch

A *Do you mind if I switch over to BBC1?*
B *Why, what's on?*
A *There's a chat show I want to see.*
B *What time does it finish?*
A *At 10.20.*
B *Well, you can watch it till 10.00. Then there's a documentary I want to see.*

a Work in pairs. Practise the dialogue.

b Using the television guide above plan exactly what you're going to watch this evening between 8.00 and 10.30. Now form groups of three or four. Try to persuade the others to watch the same programmes as you using phrases like these:

How about watching . . . ?

I'd | *rather* *prefer to* | *watch . . .*

Why don't we
Don't you want to | *watch . . . ?*
Can't we

3 🔊 News headlines

Listen to the news headlines on the radio and then answer the following questions:

1 What is the rate of inflation at the moment?
2 What does the Government expect next month?
3 How many cruise line passengers were rescued?
4 Which country did the cruise liner come from?
5 What was the nationality of most of the passengers?
6 When was the traffic jam on the M25?
7 Why do the police expect further jams between junctions 20 and 23 this evening?
8 In which part of the country were the highest temperatures yesterday?
9 What was the highest temperature, in Fahrenheit?
10 What month is it?

4 Newspaper search

Before the lesson, buy four national newspapers (two copies of a quality newspaper, for example, *The Independent* or *The Times* and two copies of a pop tabloid, for example, *The Sun* or *The Daily Mirror*).

a Form two teams. Each team has two newspapers (one quality paper and one tabloid). Half of the team looks at the quality paper, the other half at the tabloid.

b Find the answers to the following questions as quickly as possible (sometimes the answer will only be in one of the papers.)

1 What was the temperature in Madrid yesterday?
2 If you are a Leo, what sort of day are you going to have today?
3 What was the value of the British pound against the American dollar yesterday?
4 What programme is on BBC1 at 9.30 tonight?

5 What is the main editorial about?
6 Is there any news about your country anwhere in the paper?
7 Name two counties who were playing against each other in cricket.
8 What is the first clue down in the crossword?
9 What was the price of BP (British Petroleum) shares yesterday?
10 Is there a recipe anywhere in the paper? If so, what's it for?
11 What is the subject of the first letter to the Editor?
12 Is the Queen doing any official duties today?
13 Who is the main character in the first strip cartoon?
14 How much is the cheapest flight from London to Paris in the Classified Ads section?
15 What is the name of one of yesterday's TV programmes reviewed in today's paper(s)?
16 Is there a competition in the newspaper? If so, what is the first prize?
17 Who is the longest obituary for?
18 Who is the first 'story' in the gossip column about?

c Compare your answers with the other team's.

d Discuss the main differences between the two newspapers.

Summary of English in situations

- talking about television and the news
- looking at British newspapers

1 Sound right

a Listen to eight people talking. Concentrate on their intonation and tone and decide how each person sounds. Then write the number of the speaker in the box next to the correct adjective.

- ☐ angry
- ☐ worried
- ☐ impatient
- ☐ friendly
- ☐ scared
- ☐ sarcastic
- ☐ surprised
- ☐ bored

b Work in pairs. Take it in turns to say the phrases and questions below in different ways. Your partner must say how you sound.

Hello!
Really?
That's great!
Do you know what the time is?
What are you doing here?

2 Work on words

a Work in teams. Try to think of as many variations based on the words in the box below, in two minutes. The words must be spelt correctly for a team to get a point.

Example: *HAPPY*

unhappy happiness happily unhappily

b Complete these sentences with the correct form of one of the words in the box.

1 Did you keep the . . . for the jumper?
2 I spent my . . . in London.
3 How many people are . . . in the company?
4 She's a very . . . teacher.
5 There are ten . . . in the next race.
6 If you try hard you'll . . .

| employ | succeed | life |
| receive | child | compete |

3 Read and think

a Read the following story carefully.

b On your own, try to think of what the third sailor wished and add the last line to the story.

c Compare your last lines in groups.

Shipwrecked

Three sailors were shipwrecked on a desert island after their ship had sunk in a storm. There was enough food on the island for them to survive but there was no way of escaping. The three sailors desperately missed their families and friends. They would have given anything in the world to be rescued, but no ship ever passed near enough for them to send a signal.

One morning, fifteen years after they were shipwrecked they found a bottle on the beach, with a cork in it. 'Let's open it,' said one of the sailors, 'there might be a message inside it.' They took the cork out and immediately a genie appeared in a big cloud of smoke.

'Thank goodness for that,' said the genie to the astonished sailors, 'I've been imprisoned in that bottle for two hundred years. How can I ever thank you? I know. You can each make one wish. You can wish whatever you want in the world, and it will immediately come true.'

After he had said that the genie disappeared in another cloud of smoke.

The three sailors looked at each other.

'I'll wish first,' said one sailor. 'Watch me!' Then he shouted, 'I wish I were back in my home town with my wife and children!'

No sooner had he spoken than there was a flash of lightning and he disappeared.

The other two sailors looked at each other in amazement.

'Now it's my turn. Watch this!' said the second sailor. He shouted at the top of his voice, 'I wish I were back in the pub in my little village with my girlfriend.'

There was another flash of lightning and the second sailor disappeared.

The third sailor looked around him sadly. It felt strange to be without his companions after so many years. He sat down on a rock and thought to himself.

'It's so lonely here on my own. I wish . . .'

There was a flash of lightning and . . .

4 Listen to this

Listen carefully to the cassette. It contains a number of short excerpts from radio programmes. In each excerpt the speaker makes a mistake. Work in pairs or small groups and decide what the mistake is and what the speaker intended to say in each case.

1 ....

2 ....

3 ....

4 ....

5 ....

6 ....

7 ....

8 ....

5 Time to talk

'Helpful' advice?

A British magazine had a competition in which readers were asked to invent misleading but humorous advice for people visiting Britain for the first time. Here are a few examples of the entries which readers sent in.

1 Women are not allowed to travel upstairs on buses. If you see a woman there, ask her politely to leave.
2 When you enter an underground train, you should shake hands with all the passengers.
3 There are very few public toilets in Britain. You should look for signs marked 'P', in side streets.
4 Never pay the price demanded for a newspaper. Friendly bargaining is the normal thing.
5 Visitors to London hotels are expected to hang their bedclothes out of the window to air.
6 If you go by taxi, the driver will be happy to give your shoes a polish while you're waiting at the traffic lights or in traffic jams. But you may have to remind him!

a Discuss the consequences of each piece of advice. Which is the funniest?

b In groups, think of similar pieces of 'helpful' advice for visitors coming to Britain for the first time.

6 Language games

Alibi

This morning Elizabeth went to talk to her father, Lord Bellamy, about something very important . . .

a Listen to their conversation and what happened after it and mark the sentences with a tick (√) or a (×).

Lord Bellamy thinks Richard wants to marry Elizabeth for her money.
Lord Bellamy was killed with a golf club.
He died at five o'clock.
Elizabeth and Richard say they were shopping in London.
They had lunch together.
They went to the theatre in the evening.

b You are going to continue the investigation. Two students, Elizabeth and Richard go out of the room. They read their instructions on page 81.

c The other students in the class are detectives. They must think of at least twenty questions to ask Elizabeth and Richard.

Examples:
What time did you leave the house?
How did you get to Cambridge?
What did you buy?
What did you eat for lunch?

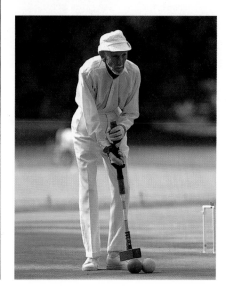

d The detectives ask Elizabeth the questions and write down her answers. They then do the same with Richard.

e If there are three or more differences in their answers, they are guilty – they killed Lord Bellamy.

7 Now you're here

The British education system

Ask a British person the following questions about education in Britain.

1 How old do you usually have to be to go to:
   a) nursery school
   b) primary school
   c) secondary school
   d) sixth form college
   e) university?
2 What's the difference between:
   a) a comprehensive and a public school?
   b) a university and a polytechnic?
3 What time do most schools start and finish?
4 How many terms are there?
5 How long are the school holidays?
6 Do all schools have a uniform?
7 Is there corporal punishment in British schools?
8 Are most schools co-educational?
9 What exams do school students take when they're 16 and 18?
10 What happens if they fail those exams? (Do they have to repeat a year?)
11 Do parents get school reports on their children?
12 Do students usually go to the university in their home town or area?
13 Do students have to pay to go to university?
14 Do most university students study a subject which trains them to do a particular job?

UNIT TWELVE · LESSON ONE

GRAMMAR IN ACTION

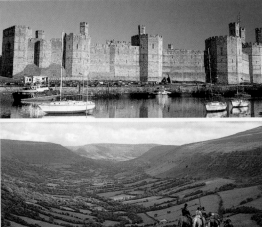

1 Looking back

a Write short answers to these questions.

b Discuss your answers in pairs or groups.

1 How did you come to Britain?

2 Were you asked any questions at Passport Control?

3 Was your luggage searched in Customs?

4 Was it your first visit? (If not, when were you here before?)

5 What surprised you most when you first arrived?

6 How long have you been here?

7 What's the weather been like?

8 What sort of things have you done in the evenings and at weekends?

9 Which trips did you enjoy the most?

10 How much money have you spent? What on, mostly?

11 Which things are much cheaper / more expensive in Britain than in your country?

12 Which of these places have you visited or been into?
   a) the doctor's
   b) a pier
   c) a cathedral
   d) a castle
   e) a sports centre
   f) a fish and chip shop
   g) the underground
   h) a Chinese takeaway
   What did you think of them?

13 If you came back to Britain where would you go? What would you do?

14 What do you think is the
best	
worst	thing about Britain?
strangest	

15 What has been your most
enjoyable	
unpleasant	experience?
embarrassing	

16 When are you leaving?

17 What's the first thing you're going to do when you get home?

18 What will you miss the most / least?

19 Are you going to write to anybody? (Who?)

20 In what ways has your opinion of Britain and the British people changed?

72

2 Noughts and crosses

a Form two teams – noughts (O) and crosses (X).

b The teacher draws this table on the board.

spelling	synonyms	prepositions
pronunciation	opposites	grammar
people	places	phrasal verbs

c Team O choose a category and the teacher asks them a question. They can discuss the question but they are only allowed one answer. If it is right the teacher rubs out the word and replaces it with an O. If the answer is wrong, the question goes to team X. If they answer correctly the teacher writes an X in that square.

spelling	synonyms	O
X	opposites	grammar
people	places	phrasal verbs

d The first team to get a straight line of X's or O's, in any direction is the winner.

3 What's the difference?

a Try to explain the difference in meaning between these pairs and groups of sentences.

b Think of other examples which make the difference in meaning clear.

1 It's a bottle   It's a milk bottle.
   of milk.

2 I'm living in Brighton.
   I live in Brighton.

3 What are you doing?
   What are you doing tonight?

4 When I arrived they went out.
   When I arrived they were going out.
   When I arrived they had gone out.

5 I'm going to post this letter.
   I'll post this letter for you, if you like.

6 How long have you worked there?
   How long did you work there?

7 I've been going out with her for two years.
   I was going out with her for two years.

8 I'll help you if I have time.
   I'd help you if I had time.

9 I used to get up early.
   I usually get up early.
   I'm used to getting up early.

10 If I knew where the party was, I'd go.
    If I'd known where the party was, I would've gone.

11 You should see that film.
    You should've seen that film.

12 He worked hard.
    He hardly worked.

13 He's gone to the bank.
    He's been to the bank.

14 Have you got a paper?
    Have you got a piece of paper?

15 I haven't had a letter from her yet.
    I still haven't had a letter from her.

16 You mustn't lock the door tonight.
    You don't have to lock the door tonight.

4 ▣ Fantastic — while it lasted

Listen to the story on the cassette and then answer these questions.

Part 1
1 What nationality was the girl?
2 Who was Hans?
3 Where in England did Karin and Mario first meet?
4 What did Karin drink?
5 Who was the taller of the two?
6 What did Mario talk about, most of the time?
7 How long was the course?
8 What did Karin not like about Mario?

Part 2
9 How did they both feel on the last day of the course?
10 Which city did Mario come from?
11 On which form of transport did they leave the course centre?
12 What month is it now?
13 What did Karin get from Mario?
14 What two things is Martin interested in?

Part 3
15 What did Mario have with him?
16 Where was Karin's mother?

1 Saying goodbye

A *Hurry up! The taxi's here!*
B *Coming!*
A *Are you sure you've got everything? Passport? Ticket?*
B *Yes, I think so. Goodbye, Mrs Harrison. Thank you very much for everything. You've been very kind to me.*
A *It was my pleasure. I just hope you've enjoyed yourself.*
B *Yes, I have. I've had a great time.*
A *Now, don't forget to write to us, will you?*
B *No, of course I won't. Will you say goodbye to Mr. Harrison for me?*
A *Yes, I will. And you give our regards to your family. Now have a good journey. Bye bye. Take care!*
B *Goodbye, and you take care of yourself, too.*

Practise the dialogue in pairs. Change roles.

2 Visiting Britain

You are going to give some advice to a foreign student, Mehmet, who is coming to Britain for the first time.

a Work in groups. Discuss the topics below and write out a list for each one.

● Five things or objects which Mehmet should bring.

Example:
an umbrella

● Five important phrases which Mehmet must learn and use.

Example:
Can I have . . . ?

● Five idioms or slang words or expressions which Mehmet should know.

Example:
You're kidding!

● Five places Mehmet should visit.

Example:
a fish & chip shop

● Five kinds of food or drink Mehmet should try or should not try.

Examples:
Try ginger beer.
Don't try baked beans.

● Five things Mehmet should do.

Example:
Have an Indian meal.

● Five things Mehmet should buy (perhaps because they're cheap in Britain).

Example:
a pair of jeans

b Compare your answers in class. Make a list of the things several groups agreed about.

3 Quick responses

a Form two teams.

b Listen to the voices on the cassette. One team at a time decide on a suitable response. You only have five seconds to answer. Score one point for a correct answer.

Example: *How are you?*
Team A *I'm fine, thanks.*

4 What would you say?

Work in teams. What would you say in each of these situations?

1 You're having dinner and your host says 'Would you like some peaches?' You can't stand them.

2 You arranged to meet a friend last night but you completely forgot. You meet him/her this morning.

3 You need to speak to your friend, Helmut, urgently. When you phone, Helmut's sister tells you that Helmut is out.

4 You want to smoke but there are other people present.

5 You are standing outside your school/centre and somebody asks you the way to the nearest post office.

6 You drop a cigarette and burn a hole in the sofa of the house where you're staying.

7 Phone the railway station. You want information about trains to and from London tomorrow.

8 You've just finished having a meal in a pizzeria. Ask for the bill.

9 When the bill arrives it seems ridiculously high. What do you say to the waiter?

10 You answer the phone. Somebody wants to speak to your friend Anna, urgently. She isn't in.

11 You bought a pair of jeans yesterday but they don't fit you. You go back to the shop where you bought them.

12 You want to come home very late this evening. Ask your host family for permission.

13 You're on a late night bus. You suddenly realize you haven't got enough money to pay the fare. The person next to you is a stranger.

14 You're at a party. You're bored and you want to leave early. What do you say to the person you're with, and to the person whose party it is?

Summary of English in situations
● saying goodbye ● giving advice to visitors to Britain

1 ▣ Sound right

a Look at these groups of words. Say them to yourself, or to the person sitting next to you.

b Decide what sound they all have in common.

Example:
sorry face city worse kiss = [s]

1 build business pretty village film
2 bought ball more born law
3 aunt calm large heart past
4 believe police seat receipt scene
5 boot lose soup rude chew
6 easy says because lazy choose
7 something birthday worth thought truth
8 goal toe shoulder although grow
9 soldier jump dangerous bridge marriage
10 question nature butcher choose lunch

c Now listen to the cassette and check if you were right.

d Think of at least two other words containing the same sounds as in 1–10 above. In pairs practise saying your words.

2 ▣ Listen to this

You're going to listen to a radio quiz show for visitors to the UK in which contestants are asked a variety of questions about Britain and the British. Listen to the questions on the cassette and write down your answers.

3 Language games

The hotel receptionist

Form two teams, A and B. All students pretend they are hotel receptionists. One student from team A comes out in front of his/her team and pretends to be a hotel guest who has lost his/her voice. The teacher gives the student a piece of paper and he/she must mime what's on the paper to the team. To get a point the team must guess exactly what the problem on the paper is. They have one minute to answer. The hotel guest cannot speak.

Example:
Student 1 *Somebody has hit you in the eye.*
Student 2 *You've seen something.*
Student 3 *You've lost your glasses.*

The game continues with a student from team B as the hotel guest.

4 Time to talk

Just a minute

a Form two teams, A and B. The teacher nominates a student from team A and chooses a subject. The student has to talk on that subject for one minute without hesitating too long or deviating from the subject.

b If any member of team B thinks that the speaker is hesitating or deviating he/she can shout out and stop the speaker. The teacher decides whether or not the challenge is correct. If it is, the student from team B has to speak on the same subject for the remaining seconds of the minute. Students from team A can now challenge him/her.

c A student scores one point for the team if he/she is speaking when the minute finishes, and five points if he/she can speak for the whole minute.

5 Work on words

Complete the sentences with the phrasal verbs below. Think carefully about word order.

see off	get on with
feel like	take after someone
get through	come round
run out of	pick someone up
break down	tell someone off
find out	

Example:
Let's go to the cinema tonight. I'll . . . (you) at 7 o'clock.

Let's go to the cinema tonight. I'll pick you up at 7 o'clock.

1 Were you really late back last night? Did your parents . . . (you)?
2 I'm sorry I'm so late. My car . . . on the motorway.
3 Could you phone the theatre for me and . . . what time the play finishes?
4 I'm tired. I don't . . . playing tennis this afternoon.
5 I don't . . . my sister. We argue all the time.
6 Are you busy tomorrow morning? Why don't you . . . for a cup of coffee?
7 I tried to phone home this afternoon but I couldn't . . . All the lines to Italy were engaged.
8 I went to the airport to . . . (my parents).
9 I can't buy any presents to take home to my parents. I've . . . money.
10 You're so like your mother. You really . . . her.

6 Now you're here

End of course quiz

Form two teams, A and B. Take it in turns to answer these questions on Britain.

1 What does the first letter on a car registration mean?

2 What do these shops sell?
   a) Etam   d) Oddbins
   b) Dolcis   e) Tesco
   c) Dixons   f) WH Smith

3 What's the smallest coin (in value) which you can use in a public phone box?

4 What's the name of the company which operates Britain's telephones?

5 Name three High Street banks.

6 What are the following?
   a) a building society
   b) an off licence
   c) an estate agent's
   d) a turf accountant's
   e) an undertaker's
   f) an Oxfam

7 Name two different kinds of British cheese.

8 Name the two main credit cards used in Britain.

9 What are the two main political parties in Britain?

10 Who is the leader of the opposition?

11 Name three soap operas currently on British television.

12 Where are the following parts of Britain?
   a) the Lake District
   b) Dartmoor
   c) the Yorkshire Moors
   d) Ulster
   e) the Isle of Wight
   f) the Channel Islands
   g) the Highlands

13 Name three London football teams.

14 How long is a yard, approximately?

15 How heavy is a pound, approximately?

16 What are the Grand National and the Derby?

17 What are the following products?
   Elastoplast   Smarties
   Andrex   Wranglers
   Biro   Typhoo
   Fosters   Phensic
   Guinness

18 What are two slang words for 'the police'?

19 How many players are there in a cricket team?

20 What's a pelican crossing?

21 What sports are normally associated with the following?
   a) Wembley
   b) Twickenham
   c) Wimbledon
   d) Brands Hatch

22 What animals are the following?
   a) a budgie
   b) a tabby
   c) a German shepherd

23 Name three British rivers.

24 Name four British counties.

25 What are the capital cities of the following?
   a) Wales
   b) Northern Ireland
   c) The Irish Republic
   d) Scotland

26 Which English county does the Channel Tunnel start from?

27 Name two places or houses lived in by members of the Royal Family.

28 What are Eton and Harrow?

29 What's the address of the British Prime Minister?

30 In which month(s) are the following
   a) St Valentine's day
   b) Guy Fawkes' day
   c) Boxing day
   d) Good Friday

31 Name three main line London stations.

32 What are the names of the two main London airports?

33 What's the leader of the Church of England called?

34 What's another name for the London Underground?

35 What's the British national flag called?

Unit 1 Lesson 3 Exercise 1 (page 10)

a Work in pairs. Student A looks at the words on page 10. Student B looks at the words below.

tea	sir	taught
true	build	said
what	half	one
foot	thank	

b Ask student A 'Which of your words rhymes with . . . ?' Take it in turns to ask and answer. Write down the rhyming pairs.

Unit 2 Lesson 3 Exercise 4 (page 16)

Work in pairs. Student A reads the instructions on page 16 and student B reads the instructions below.

Look at the picture below. Student A has a similar picture but with ten differences. Describe your picture to student A. Student A will describe his/her picture to you. Try to find the ten differences.

Unit 3 Lesson 2 Exercise 2 (page 20)

Work in pairs. Student A reads the instructions on page 20. Student B reads the instructions below.

Situation 1

You've got a foreign student staying with you. He/She is going to ask your permission to do various things.

- You don't mind him/her inviting friends to your house, but not too many.
- You don't really like other people using your kitchen.
- There's a TV programme you want to watch this evening. The stereo's in the same room as the television.

Don't be too negative!

Situation 2

You're a foreign student staying with an English family. You've been invited to a party.

- You want to miss the evening meal at home.
- You want to make some sandwiches and sausage rolls for the party.
- You want to come home late.
- You want to borrow a bike.

Ask permission. Be diplomatic – don't ask for everything at once.

Unit 7 Lesson 2 Exercise 3 (page 44)

Student A's instructions
You want to spend as much time as possible in Scotland. Try to persuade your friends to come with you by train.

Unit 3 Lesson 2 Exercise 6
(page 21)

Work in pairs. Student A reads the information on page 21. Student B reads the information below.

Your friend (A) works in the city centre, near the concert hall. You live far away. You gave A £20 yesterday to buy you a ticket to a rock concert. You've been looking forward to it for months.

Use these phrases when he/she tells you the bad news:

It's	all right.	Don't	
That's	OK.	Not to	worry.

It doesn't matter.
Never mind.

Unit 5 Lesson 2 Exercise 3
(page 32)

Work in pairs. Student A reads the instructions on page 32. Student B reads the instructions below.

Situation 1

You are Chris's brother/sister. Chris is out at the moment. You know that Chris is going to a party tonight. If somebody phones you must take a message. Make sure you get the message right.

Make sure you get:

- the place where the party is (spelt correctly)
- the meeting place and time
- the friend's telephone number.

Situation 2

You are Alex. When your friend phones you must give him/her some information about Sam, one of your friends.

Sam Akaboosi
Flat 3, 15 Carlisle Terrace
Greenwich, London SE10 9BG
Tel: 01 858 7095

Unit 6 Lesson 2 Exercise 6
(page 39)

Work in pairs. Student A reads the instructions on page 39 and Student B reads the instructions below.

Situation 1

You are the manager in charge of customer complaints in a clothes shop. You are tired of hearing the same stories. People will say anything to change something. There's someone in the shop now who wants to speak to you.

Situation 2

You want to buy a nice sweater, preferably light blue and not too expensive. Tell the sales assistant exactly what you want. Don't forget to try it on.

Unit 7 Lesson 1 Exercise 7
(page 43)

If most of your answers were a) you are sensible, responsible, loyal but perhaps a bit dull.

If most of your answers were b) you are optimistic and fun-loving but maybe you think more about yourself than other people.

If most of your answers were c) you are shy, sensitive and easily hurt. Perhaps you find it difficult to make decisions.

If most of your answers were d) you are hard-working and ambitious but perhaps you place too much importance on material things.

Unit 7 Lesson 2 Exercise 3
(page 44)

Student B's instructions
You're 21 and you've got a driving licence. Try to persuade your friends to share a hired car with you.

Unit 7 Lesson 2 Exercise 7
(page 45)

Work in pairs. Student A reads the instructions on page 45. Student B reads the instructions on this page.

Student A is going to ask you for information which you can answer by looking at the train timetable on the right.

You want to find out the following information from Passenger Travel Enquiries (Student A). Take it in turns to ask and answer.

1 You live in Newton Abbot. You want to go to London on Saturday, arriving at midday at the latest. Which train do you have to take? What time does it get to London?

2 You live in Plymouth and you want to go to Taunton on a weekday afternoon, arriving no later than 4 o'clock. Which train do you take? What time does it get to Taunton? Is there a restaurant car on that train?

3 You want to go from Totnes to Reading, arriving before 10 o'clock in the morning because you want to catch a plane from Heathrow airport. What time does the train leave Penzance? What sort of train is it? What time does it get to Reading?

Weston-super-Mare - Bristol - Bath - Swindon - London

Mondays to Fridays	125	125	125	125	125	125	125	125	125	125	125	125	125	125
Weston-super-Mare	—	—	0655	0735	0838	0920	1118	1258	1357	1543	1652	—	1848	2140
Bristol Temple Meads	—	0646	0722	0807	0920	1020	1140	1340	1440	1605	1730	—	1925	2200
Bristol Parkway	0519											1806		
Bath Spa	—	0658	0734	0819	0934	1032	1152	1352	1452	1617	1742	—	1937	2214
Chippenham	—	0709	0745	0830	0945	1043	1203	1403	1503	1628	1753	—	1948	2225
Swindon	0546	0724	0800	0845	1000	1058	1218	1418	1518	1643	1808	1833	2003	2240
Didcot Parkway						1115	1235	1435	1535	1700	1825		2020	2257
Reading (arrive) ✈	0612	0750	—	0911	1026	1128	1248	1448	1548	1713	1838		2033	2310
Slough (arrive)	0705	—		1005		1142		1502	1602	1727			2136	0005
London Paddington	0640	0820	0850	0939	1054	1200	1316	1520	1620	1745	1906	1921	2103	2339

KEY ✗ Restaurant-Buffet-Bar ⊘ Buffet-Bar IC InterCity train R Seat reservations essential
✈ Railair direct links with Heathrow and Gatwick airports
Light printed timings indicate connecting service

Unit 7 Lesson 3 Exercise 5 (page 47)

Work in pairs. Student A reads the instructions on page 47 and student B reads the instructions on this page.

Look at the pictures below. You have half of a story. Student A has the other half. Your pictures are not in the correct order. Describe your pictures to student A. Student A will describe his/her pictures to you. Try to put all ten pictures in the correct order. Then tell the story between you. You must not look at student A's pictures.

Unit 7 Lesson 2 Exercise 3

(page 44)

Student C's instructions
You haven't got much money. Try to persuade your friends to come with you on an express coach.

Unit 7 Lesson 3 Exercise 6
(page 47)

Work in pairs. Student A looks at the words on page 47. Student B looks at the words below.

Try to find words which can mean the same or almost the same as the words on your list. Write down the pairs of synonyms.

Take it in turns to ask and answer. Student A begins.

Example:
Student A *Have you got a word which can mean the same as 'reply'?*
Student B *Yes, I think it's 'answer'.*

irritate	answer	ruin
transport	frighten	commence
chase	injure	lift
insist	persuade	help
grab	repair	confess
purchase	attach	select
construct	strike	

Unit 10 Lesson 1 Exercise 3
(page 61)

Work in pairs. Student A reads the instructions on page 61. Student B reads the instructions below.

a There are ten gaps in this description of the Royal Pavilion in Brighton. Write ten questions to ask student A to find out the missing information.

Example:
What was the Royal Pavilion originally?

b Ask student A your questions and answer his/her questions.

The Royal Pavilion was originally a small (1) . . . In 1784 it was bought by George III's son, (2) . . . Then, bit by bit, it was expanded into one of the most extraordinary buildings in Britain.

In (3) . . . extra rooms were added so the house was big enough for the Prince's wild parties. In the early years of the (4) . . . more rooms and wings were added in all directions and the main rooms were redecorated in a (5) . . . style. Then, in 1805, plans were made to change the whole exterior to a Chinese style. At the last minute these plans were changed and an Indian style was decided on instead because at that time India and all things Indian were fashionable (India was then the jewel in the British Empire.)

Between 1808 and 1815 (6) . . . and stables were built and two huge new rooms were added, all in the new Indian style. This final change of style was designed by John Nash, the architect of (7) . . . A lot of new technology was used in the construction of the Pavilion and it was the first building in the world to be lit by gas. It was also centrally heated which, at the time, was revolutionary.

When the Prince of Wales became George IV in (8) . . . , he was 58 and very overweight and the Royal Pavilion was used less and less. He died 10 years later.

In the 1840's most of the (9) . . . of the Pavilion were sold and the building was nearly (10) . . . It wasn't until the 1920's that it began to be restored and its contents bought back.

Unit 7 Lesson 2 Exercise 3

(page 44)

Student D's instructions
You've got very little money. Try to persuade your friends to hitch-hike with you.

Unit 10 Lesson 2 Exercise 3
(page 63)

Work in pairs. Student A reads the instructions on page 63. Student B reads the instructions below.

Student A is going to phone you up and invite you to various things. You're not very interested in B but you don't want to hurt his/her feelings. Make excuses not to go until he/she invites you to a concert you particularly want to go to. Then arrange a time and place to meet.

Use phrases like:

No thanks, I'm afraid . . .
No, I'm sorry, I . . .
No, I've got to . . .
I've promised to . . .

Unit 11 Lesson 3 Exercise 6
(page 71)

Instructions for Elizabeth and Richard

The police think that you two murdered Lord Bellamy yesterday afternoon at 4 o'clock. You have already told them that you went shopping in Cambridge, had lunch and saw a film.

Prepare your story of what you did. The police will interview you, one at a time. You must try to tell *exactly* the same story. They will ask you questions like:

What time did you leave the house?
How did you get to Cambridge?
What did you buy?
What did you eat for lunch?

If there are three or more differences in the story you tell the police, then *you* killed Lord Bellamy!

Unit 1

Present simple v present continuous

Use the present simple when you talk about what people do all the time, or again and again.

Example:
Thousands of foreign students visit Britain every year.

You can also use the present simple when you talk about things in general which are always true, when time is not important.

Example:
Tourists say that the British are very friendly.

Use the present continuous when you talk about what is happening now, at this moment, or at the present time.

Examples:
What are you looking for?
I'm staying with an English family.

You can also use the present continuous to talk about future plans or arrangements.

Examples:
What are you doing tonight?
What time are you coming home?

Some verbs are not normally used in the present continuous, for example, the verbs *know, love, like, agree.* You cannot say 'I'm knowing her.'

Adverbs of frequency (*always, sometimes, never, etc.*)

Adverbs of frequency usually go before the main verb.

Example:

The weather	*always* *usually* *often* *sometimes* *hardly ever* *never*	*changes.*

However, adverbs of frequency come after the verb *to be.*

Example:

They're	*always* *usually* *often* *sometimes* *hardly ever* *never*	*friendly.*

Unit 2

somebody, anybody, something, anything, etc.

A number of words begin with *some* or *any*. Use them like this:

somebody, anybody someone, anyone	about people

something, anything	about things

somewhere, anywhere	about places

Use these words in the same way as *some* and *any*. In positive sentences use *somebody, someone, something* or *somewhere.*

Example:
Someone you know has bought something expensive to wear for a party.

In negative sentences and in questions use *anybody, anyone, anything* or *anywhere.*

Example:
I didn't know anybody at the party.
Would you give him anything?

Use the words *nobody* and *no one* about people. Use *everything* and *nothing* about things.

Note that you can use *something* in questions when you are making an offer or a request.

Examples:
Would you like something to drink?
Could you get me something to eat?

have to, don't have to, had to

Use *have (got) to* when you talk about things it is necessary to do or which you are obliged to do.

Present

Affirmative	Negative	Questions
have/has to	*don't/doesn't have to*	*Do you have to/* *Does he have to?*

Past

Affirmative	Negative	Questions
had to	*didn't have to*	*Did you/he have to . . . ?*

Examples:
I have to wear clothes from the shop.
I had to wear a uniform until I was 16.

Unit 3

Past simple v past continuous

Use the past simple about things which happened and finished in the past.

Use the past continuous when you talk about something which was happening over a period of time in the past.

Examples:
The children were playing in the garden.
I was watching them from my window.

You can also use the past continuous about something which was already happening when something else stopped or interrupted it (past simple).

Example:
As he was walking out of the shop, five pairs of hands grabbed him.

The past perfect

When you are already talking about the past you use the past perfect (*had* + past participle) to talk about something which had happened even earlier. In other words, for the earlier of two events in the past.

Example:
One of the workmen realized (past simple) *they had forgotten* (past perfect) *something.*

Indirect (or reported) speech

You use indirect or reported speech when you write down or tell another person what somebody else said.

Example:
'I'm a store detective.' (direct speech)
He said he was a store detective. (indirect speech)

When you change from direct to indirect (reported) speech, the tenses change like this:

Direct speech	Indirect speech
Present simple *'I work.'*	Past simple *He said he worked.*
Present continuous *'I am working.'*	Past continuous *He said he was working.*
Past simple *'I worked.'*	Past perfect *He said he had worked.*
Past continuous *'I was working.'*	Past perfect continuous *He said he had been working.*
Present perfect simple *'I have worked.'*	Past perfect simple *He said he had worked.*
Present perfect continuous *'I have been working.'*	Past perfect continuous *He said he had been working.*
Future: going to *'I am going to work.'*	'Future in the past' *He said he was going to work.*
Future: will *'I will work.'*	Future: would *He said he would work.*

Note that the structures have been written out in full but would normally be contracted in speech, *I'm, I've,* etc.

Some other words also change when you change from direct to indirect speech.

Example: direct speech   indirect speech
'I am arresting you.'   *He said he was arresting him.*

Unit 4

much, many, a lot of, a little, a few, hardly any, plenty of

Countable nouns

- Positive sentences: *a lot of, a few, hardly any, plenty of*

  Examples:
  I eat a lot of crisps.
  I have a few cans of lager.

- Negative sentences: *(not) many*

  Example:
  She doesn't eat many sweets.

- Questions: *many*

  Example:
  How many eggs do you eat?

Uncountable nouns

- Positive sentences: *a lot of, a little, hardly any, plenty of*

  Examples:
  I have a little sugar.
  I drink hardly any alcohol.

- Negative sentences: *(not) much*

  Example:
  She doesn't drink much coffee.

- Questions: *much*

  Example:
  How much tea does she drink?

Note: in spoken English *a lot of* is often used in negative sentences and questions.

Question tags

Use question tags when you want to be sure that the person you are speaking to agrees with you. When you say something positive (+), make the question tag negative (−).

Examples: +   −
That's all right, isn't it?
We've met before, haven't we?

GRAMMAR SUMMARY

When you say something negative, the question tag is positive.

Examples: –   +
You're not hungry, are you?
He didn't drink much, did he?

Unit 5

Comparatives of adjectives

- One syllable adjectives: add -er.

  Example:
  The choice of programmes is becoming wider.

  Note that adjectives ending in a single consonant (following a vowel), double the consonant: *big – bigger.*

- Two syllable adjectives: add -er or more.
  Adjectives ending in er/le/ow/y add -er.

  Example:
  My brother's cleverer than me.

  Note that adjectives ending in y change their spelling like this: *pretty – prettier, easy – easier.*
  Adjectives ending in any other letters usually form the comparative with *more. Less* is used with all two syllable adjectives.

  Example:
  Please be more careful with your spelling.

- Adjectives with three or more syllables: add *more* or *less*.

  Example:
  British soap operas are more realistic and less glamorous than American soaps.

Irregular comparatives

good	better
bad	worse

Superlatives of adjectives

- One syllable adjectives: add *the* -est.

  Example:
  They've climbed the highest mountains in the USA.

- Two syllable adjectives: add *the* -est or *the most/least*.
  Adjectives ending in er/le/ow/y add *the* -est.

  Example:
  My brother's the cleverest student in his class.

Note that adjectives ending in y change their spelling like this: *pretty - prettiest, easy - easiest.*
Adjectives ending in any other letters usually form the superlative with *the most* or *the least*.

Example:
It's the most tragic film I've seen.

- Adjectives with three or more syllables form the superlative with *the most* or *the least*.

Example:
The most popular programmes are soap operas.
The least popular programmes with women are sports programmes.

Irregular superlatives

good	the best
bad	the worst

Unit 6

Present perfect (simple and continuous) v past simple

Use the present perfect simple:

- to talk about about things which happened in the past but which still have an effect in the present.

  Examples:
  I've brought my video camera.
  I've lost my car keys.

- with *just, yet, already, never* and *ever*.

  Examples:
  The bridge hasn't opened yet.
  I've already climbed enough steps for one day!

Use the present perfect continuous:

- to talk about something which continued for some time in the past and has just stopped or is still continuing. The action still has an effect or a result in the present.

  Examples:
  I've been working very hard.
  It's been raining for hours.

Use both forms of the present perfect with *for* and *since*.

  Examples:
  How long have you been waiting?

| I've been waiting here | since 11 o'clock. |
| | for twenty minutes. |

| We've known each other | since 1986. |
| | for three years. |

Use the past simple:

- about things which happened in the past and are finished.

  Examples:
  The fire started in a baker's shop in 1666.
  I climbed the Monument this morning.

Unit 7

The second conditional

Use *if* + the past simple (*If I saw an angry bull . . .*) to talk about things which are possible but not very probable. Then use *would* + a main verb for the result (*. . . I'd run.*)
In other words, '*If A happened, B would happen.*'

You can start the sentence with '*B would happen*' and follow it with '*if A happened*'. The meaning of the sentence is the same.

Example:
I'd use my handbrake if my brakes failed.
or *If my brakes failed, I'd use my handbrake.*

Unit 8

Relative pronouns: who, which and whose

Use *who* when you talk about people.

Example:
The milkman is the person who delivers milk to your doorstep.

Use *which* when you talk about things and animals.
Example:
Summer is the season which sometimes comes to Britain.

You can usually use *that* instead of *who* or *which*.

Example:
Cricket is a game that the English invented.

The possessive form of the relative pronouns is *whose*. You can use it about people, animals or things.

Example:
Cricket is a game whose rules are impossible to understand.

usually, used to, be used to, get used to

- *usually* refers to present habits.

  Example:
  British tea is usually made with teabags and milk.

- *used to* refers to past habits or things which people did in the past but not now. It is followed by the infinitive without *to*.

  Example:
  Gardening used to be the most popular hobby (but it isn't now).

- *be used to* is completely different from *used to*. If you say that you are used to something it means that it is not strange to you, that it is familiar to you.

  Example:
  British people are used to British summers.
  Milkmen are used to getting up early.

  Use a noun, a noun phrase or an *-ing* form after *be used to*.

- *get used to* refers to the process of becoming familiar with something or making a habit of something.

  Example:
  Visitors to Britain soon get used to driving on the 'wrong' side.

  Use a noun, a noun phrase or an *-ing* form after *be used to*.

The definite article: the

Do not use *the* with nouns in the plural if you are speaking generally and are not just referring to a special group.

Examples:
British people love gardens.
(Not, 'The' British people love 'the' gardens.)

Use *the* if you are being specific.

Examples:
The people next door are always in the garden.
The milk is in the fridge.

Do not use *the* with uncountable nouns when the meaning is general, not specific.

Example:
Milk is good for you. (Not, 'the' milk)
Most pop songs are about love. (Not, 'the' love)

Unit 9

The gerund

The gerund is the verb + *ing*.

Use the gerund:
- after certain verbs, for example:
  love, hate, enjoy, like, mind, go on, stop, avoid, keep.

  Example:
  He avoided looking her in the eye.
  Keep watching the other person.

- after certain common expressions, for example:
  can't help   can't stand   it's no use/it's no good

  Example:
  It's no use trying to hide your feelings.

- after prepositions

  Examples:
  He looked at her without blinking.
  He improved his appearance by touching his hair.

Use the infinitive with *to* after most verbs.

Examples:
He wanted to know if she liked him.
She seemed to have large pupils in her eyes.

Use the infinitive with *to* when you give the reason for doing something.

Example:
He leaned forward to talk to her.

Use the infinitive without *to* after certain verbs:
can, must, may, should, might, make, let, etc.

Examples:
Just let your body talk!
You can't hide what you really feel.

Use the infinitive with *to* in the following pattern:

   verb + object + infinitive.
If you want   somebody to know that you like them.
He told   me   not to smoke.

The most common verbs used with this pattern are:
want, ask, tell, expect, invite, help, like, teach.

Unit 10

The passive

Form the passive with the verb *to be* + the past participle.

Present simple passive:

Examples:
Brighton is visited by thousands of holiday-makers.
Brighton's language schools are attended by thousands of foreign students.

Present continuous passive:

Example:
Dozens of foreign languages are being spoken.

Past simple passive:

Example:
Brighton was made fashionable by the Royal family.

Present perfect passive:

Example:
The town has been invaded by day trippers.

Future passive:

Example:
Brighton will be left in peace.

Unit 11

Third conditional

Use *if* + the past perfect (*If he had accepted the first offer . . .*) to talk about things which did not happen in the past. Then use *would(n't) have* + a main verb for the probable result (*his whole life would have been very different*). In other words, *If A had happened, B would have happened.*

Example:
If Nick hadn't been passing, Sharon would have been killed.
or *Sharon would have been killed if Nick hadn't been passing.*

You can start the sentence with *B would(n't) have happened* and follow it with *if A had(n't) happened.* The meaning of the sentence is the same.

should(n't) have . . .

Use *should(n't) have* + the past participle when you want to criticize someone or say that you are sorry about something.

Example:
The baby shouldn't have been alone on the balcony.
I should have kept her inside.

must have

Use *must have* + past participle to express a logical conclusion, or deduction about the past.

Example:
You must have been exhausted after running the marathon.

Irregular verbs

Verbs which are the same in all three forms.

Present	Past	Past participle
cost	cost	cost
hit	hit	hit
put	put	put
read [riːd]	read [red]	read [red]
shut	shut	shut

Verbs which have the same form for the past simple and the past participle.

Present	Past	Past participle
bring	brought	brought
build	built	built
buy	bought	bought
catch	caught	caught
find	found	found
get	got	got
have	had	had
hear	heard	heard
keep	kept	kept
leave	left	left
lose	lost	lost
make	made	made
meet	met	met
say	said	said
sell	sold	sold
send	sent	sent
sit	sat	sat
sleep	slept	slept
teach	taught	taught
tell	told	told
think	thought	thought

Verbs which have the same form for the present and the past participle.

Present	Past	Past participle
come	came	come
run	ran	run

Verbs which have all forms different.

Present	Past	Past participle
be	was/were	been
begin	began	begun
break	broke	broken
choose	chose	chosen
do	did	done
eat	ate	eaten
forget	forgot	forgotten
freeze	froze	frozen
give	gave	given
go	went	gone
hide	hid	hidden
know	knew	known
see	saw	seen
sink	sank	sunk
speak	spoke	spoken
steal	stole	stolen
take	took	taken
write	wrote	written

WORDLIST

UNIT 1

foreign
stranger
cool
cloudy
fed up (with)
changeable
hardly
character
complain
reserved
distant
calm
controlled
dramatic
dial
rarely
disgusting
habit
breathe
light up
relaxed
rule
privacy

UNIT 2

sales assistant
branch
suppose
advertisement
full
store
allowance
discount
envy
in fashion
bouncer
dinner jacket
bow tie
over-excited
aggressive
torn
messed-up
jewellery
loose
customer
escort (v)
sixth form
strict
mini-skirt
high heels
straight
stylish

This list contains the new, active vocabulary introduced in the first lesson of each unit. The words are listed in the order in which they appear in the text.

UNIT 3

experienced
shoplifter
department store
several
grab
contain
shirt
receipt
changing room
free
admit
steal
arrest
comment
thief
training course
store detective
stand a chance
exit
resident
old people's home
local
owner
fence
agree
lorry
realize
gap
in charge (of)

UNIT 4

diet
van
crisps
vinegar
couple
junk food
chips
hot dog
take–away
healthy
can (n)
lager
yoghurt
convenience food
frozen
quiche
vegetarian
high–fibre
wholemeal

fatty
insurance clerk
treat
doughnut
suck
'meat and two veg'
fast food
proper
pint

UNIT 5

obsession
average
soap opera
estimated
glamorous
portray
violent
opinion poll
indicate
viewer
attitude
advert
commercial
in favour (of)
commercial break
cable TV

UNIT 6

step
gallery
dome
whisper
brick
construction
disappointed
freeze
monument
hollow
column
design
commemorate
baker
exhausted
amazing

UNIT 7

skid
sink (v)
field
bull
pick up
hitch-hiker
brake
fail
forest
snake
pan
catch fire
petrol
desert
trap

UNIT 8

traditional
cereals
porridge
fried
kippers
marmalade
nowadays
grab
rush off
complicated
virtually
latest
headline
water (v)
weed (v)
century
fortunately
unfortunately
wrapped
choice
grumble
consume
standstill

UNIT 9

hide
actually
particular
sign
body language
blink
pupil
improve
appearance
touch
lean
stomach
chest
avoid

contact
fold
cross
sideways
keep your distance
backwards
point
knee

UNIT 10

to be situated
coast
fashionable
century
unique
seaside resort
holiday–maker
attend
guest
bed and breakfast
invade
crowd
day tripper
deckchair
hire
seafront
tube
sun cream
optimistic
portion
serve
sun–bather
amusement arcade
pier
fortune
genuine
gypsy
fortune teller

UNIT 11

scream
hang
terrified
balcony
rescue
horrified
grip
dive
shocked
unhurt
spokesperson
modestly
goalkeeper
lately
save
season
break (n)
advertisement
drummer

available
offer

UNIT 12

search
mostly
strangest
unpleasant
embarrassing
miss